MAGIC REALISM

LATIN AMERICAN STUDIES
VOLUME 5

GARLAND REFERENCE LIBRARY OF THE HUMANITIES
VOLUME 1675

LATIN AMERICAN STUDIES
DAVID WILLIAM FOSTER, *Series Editor*

Magic Realism
Social Context and Discourse

María-Elena Angulo

Garland Publishing, Inc.
New York and London
1995

Library of Congress Cataloging-in-Publication Data

Angulo, María-Elena.
    Magic realism : social context and discourse / by María-Elena Angulo.
        p.   cm. — (Garland reference library of the humanities ; vol.
    1675. Latin American studies ; vol. 5)
    Includes bibliographical references (p.   ) and index.
    ISBN 0-8153-1183-4 (alk. paper)
    1. Spanish American fiction—20th century—History and criticism.
2. Magic realism (Literature)   I. Title.   II. Series: Garland reference
library of the humanities ; vol. 1675.   III. Series: Garland reference library
of the humanities. Latin American studies ; vol. 5.
PQ7082.N7A76   1995
863—dc20   94-35674
                                                                    CIP

Printed on acid-free, 250-year-life paper
Manufactured in the United States of America

To my parents

SERIES PREFACE

The monographs in Garland's Latin American Studies series deal with significant aspects of literary writing, defined broadly and including general topics, groups of works, or treatments of specific authors and movements. Titles published have been selected on the basis of the originality of scholarship and the coherency of the theoretical underpinnings of the critical discourse. Cognizant of the fact that literary study is an ongoing dialogue between multiple voices, established topics and approaches complement attempts to revise the canon of Latin American literature and to propose new agendas for their analysis. Studies will also focus on interdisciplinary approaches, the bridging of national and linguistic divisions, subaltern studies, feminism, queer theory, popular culture, and minority topics. The series includes only studies written in English.

David William Foster

CONTENTS

Acknowledgments

This project began originally with funding for travel from The Center for Latin American Studies at Berkeley and the Tinker Foundation (Summer 1986), research funds from The Humanities Graduate Research Grants of the University of California at Berkeley (Summer 1986), and a fellowship from the American Association of University Women (AAUW) (1987-88) when most of the writing was done. Final writing was completed during a semester leave (Spring 1994) funded by the NYS/UUP Affirmative Action Committee.

A short version of Alicia Yánez Cossío's *Bruna, soroche y los tíos* (second part of the fourth chapter) was presented at a SUNY Conversation in the Disciplines, April 19-20, 1990 and was published in the subsequent proceedings *Translating Latin America* (Binghamton: Center for Research in Translation, 1991).

Several colleagues and friends have read chapters at one stage or another of the work and have offered valuable advice and criticism. Thanks to: Francine Masiello, Gwen Kirkpatrick, Marie-Hélène Huet, Eric Johannesson, Carole Lambert, Humberto E. Robles, Francisco Javier Cevallos, Antonio Carreño, María Lidia Spinelly, and David William Foster.

Introduction

> Criticism is a metaphor for the act of reading, and this act is itself inexhaustible. (Paul de Man, *Blindness and Insight*)

Magical realism is a well-known characteristic of the modern Latin American novel. It attempts to create "new realities" or to treat the existing ones with a different perspective from that of the social realism of the 1930s. Magical realism as a theoretical problem has occupied critics in Latin America especially after the 1950s. Alejo Carpentier, Miguel Angel Asturias, and Gabriel García Márquez are considered to be the initiators of this mode in the new novel, which attracted the attention of international critics with the so-called boom of Latin American fiction. Magical realism, however, was already present in the narrative of the 1930s. I shall show in the third chapter that José de la Cuadra's *Los Sangurimas* (1934) already has the elements which will be developed and elaborated by the "boom" writers.

This study explores how *realismo maravilloso* is used in five modern Latin American novels: Alejo Carpentier's *El reino de este mundo* (1949) and Gabriel García Márquez's *Cien años de soledad* (1967) are considered to be the canonical texts of this mode. José de la Cuadra's *Los Sangurimas* (1934), already mentioned, has several of the characteristics prized by critics in the "new novel." Demetrio Aguilera Malta's *Siete lunas y siete serpientes* (1970) dynamically presents the complexity of the social structure as the eternal question of good and evil, using an innovative narrative technique and linguistic experimentation. Alicia Yánez Cossío's *Bruna, soroche y los tíos* (1972) addresses different social issues and treats the social condition of women from the time of the Spanish conquest to the present.

In all of the above-mentioned works *realismo maravilloso* will be considered as a type of narrative discourse which is specific to Latin America due to the way it helps to elucidate social problems of race, class and gender.

I shall review first the different instances in which writers and theoreticians of Latin America have used the terms: magical realism, the fantastic, "lo real maravilloso," *realismo maravilloso*, "realismo mágico-maravilloso" and others. Magical realism is the most commonly used. I have chosen to use *realismo maravilloso* due to poetic reasons appropriate for literary analysis. I shall address these reasons in subsequent pages when Chiampi's theory is studied. This study will not give a complete account of the variation of this term; rather, it will concentrate on the more significant uses helpful towards defining a theory for the new Latin American narrative.

I shall consider first the European origins of the term in 1925 and its use by Latin American writers during the 1940s when a new aesthetic vision of reality was portrayed in fiction. Literary criticism of this period is marginal; its main focus is the thematic, the ontological and the phenomenological use of the term. Second, from the 1950s on, the term becomes popular in academic use. During the 1950s theoretical premises are still insufficient and do not equate to the already existing sophisticated narrative. In the 1970s the XVI "Congreso internacional de literatura iberoamericana" at East Lansing, Michigan, was dedicated especially to this subject. At this time, a few works presented some formal considerations; however, some did not address both aspects of the oxymoron—the real and the marvelous, while others only characterized the content of the magicorealist narratives. (From the works presented in this Congress I shall consider only those significant to this study.) Finally, in the 1980s two extensive works on magical realism were published, a semiological study by Irlemar Chiampi, and a hermeneutical one by Graciela Ricci. These works permit analyzing the problem with theoretical rigor. My review of literature on this subject emphasizes these last two works of the eighties because they go beyond the thematic-mimetic aspects; they study marvelous realism as a phenomenon of the poetic language and provide elements for a solid literary analysis. Marvelous realism can thus be applied to the text as a narrative discourse. I favor Chiampi's study, for it allows a full use of the rhetorical and discursive premises of marvelous realism. The relations of narrator, narratee, and cultural context are indispensable for our understanding of contemporary Latin American narrative.

Through presenting the critical issues surrounding marvelous realism and by analyzing literary texts from the 1930s, I illustrate the function of *realismo maravilloso* as a new way of writing which transcends the limits of the fantastic by entering the social realm. My selection of works responds to a dual purpose, first to open a wider vision for the reader, going from the well known works of Carpentier in the 1940s and García Márquez in the 1960s to explore novels of lesser known writers such as the Ecuadorians De la Cuadra in the early 1930s, and Aguilera Malta and Yánez Cossío in the 1970s who use similar techniques in their texts. By doing this I call attention to the complexity and sophistication of noncanonical works. My second objective is to acknowledge that writers since the 1930s have been using *realismo maravilloso* as a mode of writing, a discourse. I shall thus propose that it is essential to acknowledge the efforts of noncanonical writers and to recognize José de la Cuadra as one of the pioneers of this discourse. For many years both canonical and noncanonical writers have used *realismo maravilloso* as a way of interpreting in fiction the highly complex Latin American reality.

Magic Realism

REALISMO MARAVILLOSO

Problem of Definition. Different Theoretical Formulations

To begin any study on marvelous realism it is necessary to start with the classic review of the first articles on this theme. In 1925, in his book *Nach-Expressionismus (Magischer Realismus)*, the art critic Franz Roh coined the term "magical realism" to refer to the objectivity of German postimpressionism.[1] He used the term as an aesthetic category, a way of representing the mystery inherent in things:

> En el post expresionismo se nos ofrece el milagro de la **existencia en su imperturbada duración**: el inagotable milagro de que las vibraciones de las moléculas—eterna movilidad—, de que el constante aparecer y desaparecer de lo existente, segregue, sin embargo, objetos permanentes; en suma, la maravilla de que el tumulto de lo variable cristalice en determinadas constantes. (qtd. in *Revista de occidente* 48 (1927): 285)

Through the Spanish translation of this book the term was probably known in Latin America and generated studies based on the phenomenological aspects which were predominant in Latin American literary criticism of the forties. On the use of the term "realismo mágico," Enrique Anderson Imbert in his article "Literatura fantástica, realismo mágico y **lo real maravilloso**," states: "Este término era muy conocido en las tertulias literarias de Buenos Aires que yo frecuentaba en mi adolecencia" (39).

What is important for our purposes is to consider that in Spanish America in the forties the term was used to express a new literature inherent to the mentality and attitude of its writers.

---

[1]For a study of magical realism as an "across-the-arts phenomenon" see the detailed and informative work by Seymour Menton, *Magical Realism Rediscovered, 1918-1981*.

It is known that Arturo Uslar Pietri first used this term to refer to the Venezuelan short stories of the thirties and forties:

> Coincidía este momento con el contagio de las formas literarias de vanguardia: cubismo francés, ultraísmo español y los primeros vagidos del surrealismo. Lo que vino a predominar en el cuento y a marcar sus huellas de una manera perdurable fue la consideración del hombre como misterio en medio de los datos realistas. Una adivinación poética o una negación poética de la realidad. Lo que a falta de otra palabra podría llamarse un realismo mágico. (Uslar Pietri 161-62)

Uslar Pietri was in Paris in the 1920s, and he was exposed to all of the new movements of the period. Although he does not mention Roh in his definition, one can assume that he was familiar with the term. His definition of the new prose, where man is a mystery among realistic data ("el hombre como misterio en medio de los datos realistas") follows the pattern of Roh's idea. There is, however, ambiguity in his definition and a double problem: one regarding the phenomenology of the perception in the narrator's attitude towards reality, the second refers to the ontology of reality (Chiampi 25). Uslar Pietri centers the importance of magical realism in the creative act, and he does not address the linguistic representation of the same in the text.

That same year (1948), the newspaper *El Nacional* published Alejo Carpentier's "De lo real maravilloso americano." This essay appeared as a prologue to the novel *El reino de este mundo*, published in Mexico in 1949. In this Prologue, he talks of his visit to Haiti and his discovery of "lo real maravilloso" when remembering the different events during the reign of Henri Christophe, the first black king in America (1807-1820). For Carpentier "lo real maravilloso" is inherent not only to Haiti but also to all Latin America where it is possible to find natural historical and cultural phenomena. Some years later Carpentier will expand this Prologue but the basic principles do not change. (See *Tientos y diferencias* 102-20. I quote the Prologue from the edition of *El reino de este mundo*, La Habana: Editorial Letras Cubanas, 1979). This is a natural marvelous, different from the one created by the artificial methods of the surrealists. For the American marvelous Carpentier presupposes faith:

> Lo maravilloso comienza a serlo de manera inequívoca cuando surge de una inesperada alteración de la realidad (el milagro), de una

revelación privilegiada de la realidad, de una iluminación inhabitual o singularmente favorecedora de las inadvertidas riquezas de la realidad, de una ampliación de las escalas y categorías de la realidad percibidas con particular intensidad en virtud de una exaltación del espíritu que lo conduce a un modo de "estado límite." Para empezar, la sensación de lo maravilloso presupone una fe. (9)

Carpentier's referential value for "lo real maravilloso americano" has been discussed and argued; however, the metaphorical value of this referent, as will be noted later, has been used to study how narrative language attempts to maintain an American identity within the Western context. Carpentier's call to Latin American writers to look to the American continent as a source of inspiration rather than to Europe coincided with the peak moment of the definition of a Latin American identity which explains the popularity of this prologue. As stated by Rodríguez Monegal in "Lo real y lo maravilloso en *El reino de este mundo*," this essay will become a kind of manifesto for the new Latin American fiction (101). After Carpentier's essay, references to the "real maravilloso" are given by different writers, Mario Vargas Llosa and Gabriel García Márquez among them as well as by several minor writers when they refer to the Latin American new narrative.

In 1954 at the Modern Language Association conference in New York, Angel Flores presented a paper entitled "Magical Realism in Spanish American Fiction." In this well-known work he discusses the appropriate use of the term "magical realism" as the "authentic expression" for the Latin American writers. The novelty for him is "the amalgamation of realism and fantasy," a tendency stimulated by Kafka and Proust and started in Latin America by Borges and Mallea. According to him, the starting point for "magical realism" would be Borges's *Historia universal de la infamia* published in 1935. Flores's broad definition of the term and the inclusion of a heterogeneity of works and writers makes this definition inaccurate. Rodríguez Monegal's article "Realismo mágico versus literatura fantástica: un diálogo de sordos," shows in detail the weaknesses of Flores's definition, especially those regarding the writings of Kafka and Borges and the broad use of "realismo" and "fantasía." Flores's article contributed to the popularity of the term in reference to the new Hispanic American narrative, but while he mentions a huge diversity of authors, who, according to him, belong to magical realism, he ignores Alejo Carpentier, whose work, which will be studied in the second chapter, is of seminal importance for this literary mode.

Twelve years later, in 1967, in "El realismo mágico en la literatura hispanoamericana," Luis Leal refuted the article of Flores. Leal disagreed with the authors included by Flores and also with the chronology established by him, and he posited Roh as the originator of the term and Uslar Pietri as the first one to use it in Hispanic America. For Leal, magical realism can be identified neither with the fantastic or psychological literature nor with surrealism, because "El realismo mágico es, más que nada una actitud ante la realidad":

> El realismo mágico no se deriva, como quiere el profesor Flores, de la obra de Kafka...no es tampoco, como el vanguardismo, una literatura de evasión... El mágico realista no trata de copiar (como lo hacen los realistas) o de vulnerar (como lo hacen los surrealistas) la realidad circundante, sino de captar el misterio que palpita en las cosas. (233-34)

Although Leal establishes the chronology of magical realism—references to Roh and Uslar Pietri, omitted by Flores—his definition is still ambiguous and vague, especially when he refers to the attitude of the writer. Leal's main contradiction is in the attitude towards reality, because, while the thesis of Roh only suggests the attitude of the author, Leal confuses it with the reaction of the characters. Nevertheless, Leal establishes the differentiation between fantastic and realistic literature which, as will be shown later, is one of the main points to be considered in the discussion of magicorealist fiction.

Arturo Fox in "Realismo mágico: algunas consideraciones formales sobre su concepto" applies to magical realism the theory of Northrop Frye on the "ironic mode" and the reappearance of myth. For Fox, the magicorealist writer does not discriminate and applies detailed realistic descriptions "democratically" to all works; the author's suspension of judgement is ontological. In fantastic literature, on the other hand, there is "ontological duality" which is exactly the opposite of magical realism. Although considering the semantic aspect of magical realism, Fox does not develop further the formal difference between the fantastic and magical realism. This difference, as it will be studied in subsequent pages, is important.

Lucía Inés Mena, first in "Fantasía y realismo mágico" and later in "Formulación teórica del realismo mágico," studies the correspondence of magical realism with the marvelous as established by Todorov in his *Introduction to Fantastic Literature*. For Mena, the central problem of magical realism is the definition of its content and the lack of unified theoretical concepts on the same. When studying the theoretical concepts, however, Mena explores only the marvelous, and does not make any reference to the real, the other important aspect of the oxymoron *realismo maravilloso*.

Floyd Merrell in "The ideal world in search of its reference: an inquiry into the underlying nature of magical realism," explores the "epistemological implications" and the nature of magical realism. Merrell uses concepts of modern anthropology, philosophy, and language (Lévi-Strauss, Langer, Cassirer). He departs from the statement made by González-del-Valle and Cabrera in *La nueva ficción hispanoamericana a través de M.A. Asturias y G. García Márquez* (1972), that new narrative in Spanish America after the thirties and forties is based on a new aesthetic vision of reality where the writer is the creator of the world of his fiction. Merrell considers that genesis and mimesis are the two poles of opposition revealed through magical realism in the Hispanic American narrative. For him, the essays on magical realism by Carpentier ("De lo real maravilloso americano"), Flores ("Magical Realism in Spanish American Fiction"), Leal ("El realismo mágico en la literatura hispanoamericana"), Valbuena Briones ("Una cala en el realismo mágico"), and Carter ("Breve reseña del realismo mágico en Hispanoamérica") disclose a "traditional" view of magical realism, while Cabrera and González-del-Valle propose a "genetic view" comparable to the twentieth century relativistic view of physical reality (9). According to Merrell, magicorealist fiction stems, on a thematic level, from the conflict between two pictures of the world, but the roots of magical realism must be searched in the linguistic medium which is the writer's way to express theme (11). He concludes that "Magical Realism, in the final analysis, must be considered a local expression whose function and structure reveal a universal epistemological phenomenon" (13).

Jaime Alazraki, in "Para una revalidación del concepto realismo mágico en la literatura hispanoamericana," also studies magical realism from an anthropological point of view. His aim is to clarify and to make suggestions about the concept of magical realism elaborated in the different works presented at the "XVI Congreso de literatura iberoamericana." Alazraki justifies the use of the term because its concept helps to understand and to explain some of the directions of the New Latin American fiction. He considers that Carpentier's proposition of "lo real maravilloso" is the one that best defines magical realism (15). In Carpentier's definition, magicorealist literature is distinguished first for its themes emerging from the American reality, and, second, for the treatment of the same. Defined by these points, only narratives governed by legend, myth and magic could be considered magicorealist. Alazraki asserts that Carpentier's idea of the faith in magical realism coincides with the propositions made by Lévi-Strauss who also asserts that for the efficacy of magic, faith is indispensable. Following this same line of coincidence, Alazraki makes the parallel of the mythical world presented by Asturias and the world of the Cunas referred to by Lévi-Strauss in his explanation of the Mu-Igala. In the world that Asturias describes, from the perspective of the Indians, witchcraft has the same force and validity for them as science has for the "civilized" world (17). We shall note this same characteristic when studying Carpentier's *El reino de este mundo*. Faith in voodoo is the main force in the slaves' revolutionary movement. Alazraki concludes that the aim of the magicorealist writer is to reformulate his fiction from magic, myth, or legend as an answer "desde la literatura, a la mutilación y negación cultural de la sociedad latinoamericana" (18).

Alazraki's attention to Carpentier's definition, to differentiate magicorealist fiction by its themes, emerging from American reality as a differentiated cultural product, where myth, legend, or magic are included, is important. Considering the rich variety of Latin American fiction it is also important to note that not all modern narrative can fall under the category of magical realism.

From the above critical studies it is clear that magical realism has been used to identify the new Latin American narrative as a break with past traditional regionalism and as a step toward the interpretative renewal which reflects the thematic and aesthetic complexity of the new narrative. However, none of the above studies presents a complete account of theoretical principles for the analysis of marvelous realism as a narrative discourse. These principles will appear in the 1980s in two extensive works: *O realismo maravilhoso. Forma e ideología no romance hispano-americano* (1980) by the Brazilian Irlemar Chiampi and *Realismo mágico y conciencia mítica en América Latina* (1985) by the Argentinean Graciela Ricci.

Realismo maravilloso as Narrative Discourse

Irlemar Chiampi in her book *O realismo maravilhoso. Forma e ideología no romance hispano-americano*. (São Paulo: Editora Perspectiva, 1980) situates the term *realismo maravilloso* both within the literary process of Hispanic America and within the "discurso del americanismo" which was one of the preoccupations of Hispanic American thinkers especially after 1925. One of the most interesting chapters of Chiampi's book is her study of the ontological and ideological preoccupation of Latin American writers to define their culture within the western context. As will be noted in subsequent pages Chiampi reviews the different moments of this discourse as "ideologemas."[2] *Realismo maravilloso* and new Hispanic American literature are studied as phenomena of poetic language, thus encompassing all discourse relations. In the words of Chiampi:

> O problema da construção poética do novo realismo hispano-americano não pode ser pensado fora da linguagem narrativa, vista em suas relações com o narrador, o narratário e o contexto cultural. (28-29)

Chiampi adopts the term *realismo maravilloso* and not "realismo mágico" due to lexical, poetical and historical advantages offered by the first term to signify the new Hispanic American narrative (48).

Chiampi rightly establishes that some of the main weaknesses in former criticism on marvelous realism are due to the phenomenological treatment of the novel that projected the problem outside the text, the inadequate understanding of Carpentier's cultural statement on "lo real maravilloso" which led to the thematic treatment of the problem, and the confusion of magical realism with fantastic literature (28-29).

Next she examines Carpentier's ideas on Latin America stated in his famous Prologue to *El reino de este mundo* on "lo real maravilloso." In this prologue, Chiampi traces the influence of surrealism, especially of Pierre Mabille's *Le miroir du merveilleux* (1962) and establishes the metaphorical importance of the same which is related to the ideology of the "discurso americanista":

> É inútil reivindicar qualquer valor referendial (sic) para o real maravilhoso americano. Seu valor metafórico, contudo, oferece um teor cognitivo que bem pode ser tomado como ponto de referência

---

[2]The term ideologeme which was coined by N.P. Medvedev in 1928 is applied by J. Kristeva to textual analysis (*Le Texte du roman* 12). I. Chiampi in *O realismo maravilhoso* (96-134) considers ideologeme to be "textual organization" but previous to its literary or poetic organization, in the sense of cultural unities which form the general cultural text. She applies it to the ideological Latin American discourse.

para indagar sobre o modo como a linguagem narrativa tenta
sustentar essa suposta identidade da América no contexto ocidental.
(39)

The principles for the "realistic marvelous narrative" are based on the
linguistic relations of the "act of codification" and the reading of the sign.

The semantic relation accounts for how the extralinguistic referent
(vertical relation) is signified within the text; the pragmatic relations are those
between the "emissor" (sender) and the sign and between the "receptor"
(receiver) and the sign—codification and decodification of the sign—(51). To
characterize this process, Chiampi contrasts *realismo maravilloso* with the
fantastic, basing her study on the theoretical principles given by Vax, Todorov,
and Bessière. Reformulating them, she arrives at the conclusion that the
fantastic is based on the "poetics of the uncertain," with disjunction of the
natural/supernatural. In *realismo maravilloso*, on the contrary, the unusual is
incorporated into reality; there is an "effect of enchantment" produced by the
nondisjunction of natural/supernatural (semantic aspect) and by the internal
causality of the narrative text (syntactic aspect) (59). Chiampi asserts that "a
causalidade interna ("mágica") do realismo maravilhoso é o fator de uma
relação metonímica entre os dados da diégese" (61).

Among the pragmatic relations of *realismo maravilloso* she focuses on the
act of enunciation. She considers the difference between "narrative mood" and
"voice" (Genette) and states that the renovation of fictional language in
Spanish America has as central axis the problematization of narrative
perspective (72). Taking note of Genette's opposition between the mimetic
and diegetic narrative mood Chiampi starts her analysis with the traditional
realistic Spanish American narrative which is characterized by the omniscient
narrator. Then she arrives at the realistic marvelous texts characterized, first,
by the metadiegesis ("o nível da narrativa que fala do relato primeiro"), which
can be implicit or explicit (79); and second, by the descriptive baroque ("o

barroquismo descriptivo"), or the multiplication or distortion of the signifier in order to describe the indescribable (85).

Chiampi uses the Bakhtinean concept of the poetic discourse which goes beyond the language system and has to be studied as a dialectical exchange, and characterizes *realismo maravilloso* as a dialogue between the sign and the extra-linguistic referent. When we qualify a fact of "real maravilloso," we are already implying "an idea" about its referent. In this sense any objective reflection on the "realistic marvelous narrative" starts on the semantic level (91). Thus, the American "real maravilloso" is a cultural unity (Schneider-Eco) which does not require as referent the physical existence of an object. It is a semantic unity inserted in a system of conventions of the Hispanic American culture (93). Within this cultural unity can be studied all the different "ideologemas" (Kristeva) of "American discourse."

Chiampi starts her study with the chronicles on the discovery of America and considers that each ideologeme comes out as the symptom of a historical crisis. The "ideologema da crônica" with the unity of "maravilha" comes at the time of the discovery of America as the "fourth dimension" of the world (Américo Vespucio). The "ideologema da Ilustração, neo-utopia" marks the degeneration of that system and the independence conspiracy; the "ideologema pós-colonial" corresponds to the time of the consolidation of the independence movements, the discourses of Bello and Bolívar; the "ideologema do positivismo" in the nineteenth century would start with Sarmiento's "América bárbara" and with "América enferma" (Alcides Arguedas and others), towards the end of the century. In the twentieth century there are the "ideologema de la América Latina" (Rodó) and the "ideologema de la América indígena" (Mariátegui); these are related to the neocolonialist policies of the United States and to leftist revolutionary ideas respectively. Finally, there is the ideologeme of "mestiçagem" which is the most important of the century. This ideologeme has the characteristic of nondisjunction; it has the idea of the American culture as a synthesis with no contradictions, a fusion of races and dissimilar cultures. This ideologeme is well expressed in the essays of the Hispanic American writers from the beginning of the twenties—Vasconcelos, Rojas, Uslar Pietri—and later around the forties and fifties with the essays by Carpentier, Paz, Lezama Lima. The one that helps to express best the real marvelous referent to the new narrative mode is Carpentier's "lo real maravilloso" due to the expressiveness of its oxymoron (110-34).

To arrive at a definition of the realistic marvelous discourse which is specific to Hispanic America for its quality of representation and experimentation, Chiampi examines the isotopies "natural" (real) and "supernatural" (unreal) in realistic, marvelous, and fantastic discourses. Basing her relations on the works of Alexandrescou and Todorov and reformulating their premises, she establishes that the characteristic of *realismo maravilloso* is the nondisjunction of contradictory terms. This discourse manifests two modalities, one that affirms and denies simultaneously the realistic code; the other, that affirms and denies the marvelous code (145); this gives the origin to "Another Sense":

> A narração tética (do realismo) e a não tética (do maravilhoso) associam-se, não já para codificar a mensagem transparente dos verossímeis exclusivos, mas para erigir Outro Sentido, inteligível no contato dialógico entre as **naturalia** e as **mirabilia**. (148)

To establish the "realistic marvelous narrative sign," Chiampi uses the semiotic principles on the homology of the poetic language. She considers the quadripartite division of the sign: substance and form of expression; substance and form of content (Hjelmslev-Dubois) to state that:

> A solidariedade e pressuposição entre a expressão e o conteúdo que Hjelmslev aponta para toda função semiótica pode ser interpretada, pois, no signo poético narrativo do realismo maravilhoso, como uma relação homológica entre o discurso e o relato. Abertos às suas respectivas grandezas substanciais, ambos apresentam um mesmo tipo de relação na não disjunção dos termos contraditórios. (163)

In the above relation verisimilitude is very important. Adopting Kristeva's concept of "verisimilar discourse" Chiampi concludes that "a 'verdade' do texto provém de um efeito interdiscursivo" (167). Regarding *realismo maravilloso*, she remarks:

> o verossímil do realismo maravilhoso consiste em buscar a reunião dos contraditórios, no gesto poético radical de tornar verossímil o inverossímil. Para legitimar esse impossível lógico, o texto aciona uma retórica específica que, em última instância, consiste em organizar, pelo efeito de semelhança, a cumplicidade entre as palavras e o universo semântico. (168-69)

Chiampi's semiological study is important because it considers the evolution of the forms of representation of the Latin American narrative.

Critics before her had identified with magic the way writers now in Latin America construct a multivalent image of reality. However, no one before her had examined to such an extent the mechanics of the construction of verisimilitude through the analysis of the signifier/signified of new narrative. As noted by França Danese in his minute review of Chiampi's book, *O realismo maravilhoso* opens new possibilities for understanding the renovation of narrative language in Latin America (46). This complex study which implies poetic elements as well as the ideology of the Latin American literary production is appropriate for analyzing current narrative.

Five years after Chiampi's study, Graciela N. Ricci in her book *Realismo mágico y conciencia mítica en América Latina* (Buenos Aires: García Cambeiro, 1985), adopts the term "realismo mágico-maravilloso" (RMM), combining the two terms proposed by earlier critics and Chiampi. According to Ricci the definition "realismo mágico-maravilloso" is:

> la más pertinente pues, además de diferenciarse, de este modo, del concepto europeo original aplicado a las artes plásticas ("Realismo Mágico") y del otro concepto europeo, estrictamente literario y alejado de la realidad ("lo maravilloso"), permite las necesarias conexiones entre una literatura y su acción fundamentalmente revolucionaria, y la conciencia de Latinoamérica; reafirmando así la convicción irrenunciable de "reconocerse en la propia palabra". (56)

Ricci studies the problematic of magical realism considering that the poetics of the Latin American narrative and its "efecto de encantamiento" (enchantment effect) are based on the structural equivalence of text and contexts. There is an analogy between the archetype consciousness of culture and the RMM narrative. Magical realism is treated as part of the Latin American cultural context and also as part of the unconscious of its writers.

The first part of Ricci's study is a diachronic analysis of the evolution of consciousness. She studies the different mythical cycles that occur in the development of every individual or collective consciousness and the symbolic function of the psyche (49). Myth, symbol of second degree (Ricoeur), is a metalanguage which refers to a sphere beyond the concepts already known (34). She traces the historical definition of the myth and the elements that contribute to form the "magic" vision of America, thus magical realism emerges as a profound expression of the spiritual evolution of American consciousness (40).

In the second part, Ricci studies the definition of magical realism in the literary text and its relation to the extratextual conceptual reality it signifies and represents. She states that marvelous realism should be studied considering: a) the reader's relation work-consciousness (pragmatic perspective) and b) the extratextual relation text-referent (semantic perspective). Both perspectives take the reader outside the text. For Ricci, the basic traits of the psyche which differentiate and define the mind of a Latin American writer from that of a European are projected by analogy in Latin American literature by this process: embryo gestation and birth; immersion in history and formation of the I; growth and maturity with mastery of language and conscience (57). The basic traits of Latin American consciousness are: recurrence of the archetypes of death and rebirth; psychological "mestizaje" as a result of an ethnic-cultural historical plurality forced to adopt a unique language and to fight against an exterior reality; facility to accept the marvelous; European, semi-Oriental, African and autochthonous mythical-religious heritage, which enrich the archetype of the collective consciousness and tend to a more affective participation of the symbols and myths intertwined in literary and extraliterary reality (59).

Ricci summarized the different archetypal-cultural stages that will end in the crisis of realism in the twentieth century, its dynamic and dialectical relation with literature. According to her, the different changes of the narrative at the present time are the peculiar way in which Latin American literature has absorbed the contradictions and the antagonistic movements of its cultural history. Ricci's aim is to describe the poetic resolution of this problematic within the narrative (60).

In the semantic relations of the magical realistic referent, Ricci, in the same way as Chiampi, adopts the quadripartite division of the sign (substance and form of the expression, substance and form of the content). Ricci proposes another subdivision within the form of the content: the archetypal form ("mitologemas" of the archetypal code) and the ideological form (cultural unities of the cultural code or "ideologemas" (Kristeva). Using the ideologemes proposed by Chiampi for Latin American narrative, and adding the "mitemas" (Lévi-Strauss) proposed by Neumann for the archetypal code, Ricci proceeds to make an analogy of both to form the extratextual Latin American referent. In the archetypal code there are three cycles: 1) the myth of creation; 2) the myth of the hero; 3) the myth of transformation. These cycles are parallel in the Historic-cultural Code to: 1) (1492-1825) Extroversion—the Discovery (Spanish chronicles), Colonization (Indian chronicles), Independence (Illustration); 2) (1825-1925) Introversion—Postcolonialism ("civilización-barbarie" Bello, Bolívar, Sarmiento), Positivism, confrontation with neocolonialism, "América Latina" (Rodó), "América Indígena" (Vasconcelos, Mariátegui); 3) first period (1925-1960)—Centroversion. Second, postwar ("mestizaje", and then "realismo mágico-maravilloso") (60-75). Ricci concludes reasserting that "realismo mágico maravilloso," rather than *realismo maravilloso* (Chiampi), is the expression that summarizes best the cultural synthesis of the Latin American narrative. According to Ricci, "realismo magico maravilloso" unites the two poles of a same psycho-intellectual reality with a nondisjunction at the semantic level (literary projection of the cultural phenomena of "mestizaje") and at the syntactic and discursive level of the text (87).

The third part is a study of the synchronic and structural aspects of magical realism. Ricci attempts to determine how the archetypal form of the expression (symmetric structure of the unconscious) blends by asymmetry in the magicorealistic-marvelous narrative discourse (91). To analyze the structure of the psyche, Ricci takes note of Ignacio Matté Blanco's study *L'inconscio come insiemi infiniti* (1981). For Matté Blanco, the homogeneous and indivisible totality (symmetric system) is previous to the heterogeneity and divisibility (asymmetric system) according to Aristotelian logic. The latter is the only one used and dominated by the Western psyche; there is a continuous personal and cultural enrichment, and the human psyche progresses and matures through time (105).

Ricci considers that Matté Blanco's reformulation of the unconscious system allows two concepts: the unconscious and mythical consciousness. She coins the term "ontoconciencia" to integrate the two (109). According to Ricci, Matté Blanco proposes to study the unconscious systematically with a logic-mathematic formulation. This approximation provides the necessary elements to analyze how and with what intensity the "metric" system of the psyche can be intertwined in the structure of the literary text. For Ricci "realismo mágico-maravilloso" is the result of a particular evolution of the Latin American consciousness. This evolution is manifested at present in some narrative works, in intermittent artistic groups and in scientific groups. She foresees, however, that through its literature and through the foundational myths of the West there is a certain future in RMM for Latin America (110). Ricci is aware that when using Matté Blanco's methodology at a literary level, many of the symmetric aspects of RMM do not have an unconscious character; she considers, however, that the deep structure of RMM has its roots in the "ontoconciencia." Ricci agrees with Matté Blanco that the characteristics of the unconscious system must be traced in the language system. When this is enriched with elements of the symmetric system, the conclusion is that the narrator expressing that language has reached, in part, the integrated zones of the "ontoconciencia":

> Y si se da el caso de que éste [el lenguaje] se halle enriquecido con profusión de elementos pertenecientes al sistema simétrico, entonces una conclusión pertinente es que el narrador que expresa ese tipo de lenguaje ha logrado contactar, al menos en parte, con las zonas homogéneas e integradoras de la Ontoconciencia. (111)

Next, she proceeds to study the characteristics of realistic, fantastic, and RMM narrative. She considers the different studies on the real, the fantastic and the marvelous (Callois, Vax, Castex, Todorov), to assert that realistic discourse would reproduce the understandable universe, with dominance of the "asymmetric" and its laws for space, time, causality, and consequences (112). Marvelous discourse would reproduce the supernatural universe, which is accepted by the reader without question. Fantastic discourse departing from a realist discourse would have its "familiar reality" irrupted by the unusual or the unknown event. Ricci mentions different critics who have made contributions to the study of the fantastic and states that she is not interested in the thematic debate but in its differentiation from realist and from real marvelous narrative (113). The literary discourse of "realismo mágico maravilloso" (RMM) with characteristics quite different from the traditional fantastic literature starts in Latin America in the 1940s (122). This discourse reflects a different dimension in the evolution of consciousness: the partial focalization of the I in the "ontoconciencia"; it intends a transformational synthesis of the natural and the supernatural with its respective counterparts nonnatural and nonsupernatural. There is an equilibrium of real and unreal isotopies; the concept of verisimilitude is modified (126). Ricci agrees with Chiampi that marvelous realism does not avoid the "realia" nor eliminate causality. The reader accepts the coexistence of both worlds by acknowledging in magic and discontinuous causality the explanation of a transcendental reality. The effect of "enchantment" of RMM includes a revisionist conception of the universe. Thus RMM is originator of Sense, implying from the ontological point of view a superior image of the cosmos, and from the phenomenological point of view a profound experience where the reader is participant of a same spiritual community (127). In RMM, the nonconflictive coexistence in the same space and time of two universes and of two modalities of existence, the absence of vacillation and the previous or simultaneous representation of the realia, calls the reader's attention to the contiguity of these two worlds: the real and the marvelous (174). Ricci shows the characteristics of fantastic narrative with an analysis of Leopoldo Lugones's "Lluvia de fuego" and exemplifies her RMM theory with an analysis of María Granata's *Los viernes de la eternidad*. According to Ricci:

> El RMM, con su "isotopía de la coincidencia", supera los movimientos dialécticos, dirigiendo el equilibrio de las dualidades hacia un Sentido Otro que trasciende las significaciones conocidas. (189)

Ricci concludes with an optimistic note for the future of Latin America and the importance of the literary work.

These two detailed studies treat the problematic of magical realism with theoretical rigor and propose a narrative discourse which permits analysis of literary texts. I favor Chiampi's study because it considers the ideology of the "discurso americanista" and the inquiry of cultural identity which has been a vital force in Hispanic American thought. It also allows the use of the rhetorical and discursive premises of marvelous realism. The relations of narrator, narratee, and cultural context are indispensable for our understanding of contemporary Latin American narrative. Ricci adds another dimension to marvelous realism, the relation to the unconscious; however, her application of Matté Blanco's logic-mathematic formulation to a literary text is problematic.

By including these two important works of the 1980s I hope to call the attention of the critics to the first detailed works on a theory to be applied specifically to Latin American texts. As far as I know there is only França Danese's book review of Chiampi's book, and I have not been able to find any review of Ricci's work. To develop a genuine theory for Latin American literary production, we need diffusion of the works and communication among critics, that is, acknowledgement of previous works, discussion of different premises and ideally collaboration on theoretical enterprises. Critics have complained about the lack of communication among intellectuals; Octavio Paz in his *Corriente alterna* (8) attributes to this fact, the dispersion of Hispanic American criticism. Rodríguez Monegal, in his opening discourse on magical realism at East Lansing, Michigan, "Realismo mágico versus literatura fantástica: un diálogo de sordos" states:

> Hace muchos años que uno de los críticos hispanoamericanos más prolíficos, don Luis Alberto Sánchez, acuñó aquello de la "intersordera" para referirse a la falta de comunicación entre los países de la

América hispánica. Hoy, podemos seguir hablando de un diálogo de
sordos. (26)

Ricci's work and her acknowledgement of Chiampi's theoretical principles
on marvelous realism seems to be an attempt to break the "intersordera." This
attempt could well be followed by others in the future. We know that for
Benveniste discourse entails reference to the enunciation and implies a sender
and a receiver (Prince 21). We also know that all speech and writing is social
and that discourses differ within and across countries (Macdonell 1). In my
analysis of the texts I use *realismo maravilloso* as a narrative discourse,
considering its rhetoric, its semantic and its discursive premises and giving
special attention to the relationship among narrator, narratee and cultural
context. In Latin American narrative, it is important to consider historical and
ideological differences and the modifications of Latin American narrative
which obey the particular cultural space from which the narrative comes.
According to Braudel, "it is from the conflict—or the harmony—between
ancient attitudes and new necessities, that each people daily forges its destiny,
its 'actuality'" (*On History* 216).

Our "actuality" in comparative literature is enriched and grows not only
from the study of past and present writers, but also from the comparison of
the writers from different countries, for comparative literature is based on the
interaction of cultures. Although we speak of Latin American culture in
general, we know that there are significant differences. Each novel can be
affected by its specific historical background, and both literature and history
influence each other; both are organized into a narrative, and both are
structured according to cultural schemes embedded in the language or in the
ideology of the time of narration. However, it is entirely up to the writer to
make use of and to choose the elements he/she considers important to create
his/her work of art—the novel. We shall observe this in the different novels
chosen for this study: Alejo Carpentier's *El reino de este mundo*, Gabriel
García Márquez's *Cien años de soledad*, José de la Cuadra's *Los Sangurimas*,
Demetrio Aguilera Malta's *Siete lunas y siete serpientes* and Alicia Yánez
Cossío's *Bruna, soroche y los tíos*. In these narratives myth intermingles with
history, all have elements of marvelous realism, yet each novel is a unique
artistic universe.

TWO CANONICAL NOVELS OF *REALISMO MARAVILLOSO*

> La única raza humana que está impedida de desligarse de las fechas es la raza de quienes hacen arte, y no sólo tienen que adelantarse a un ayer inmediato, representado en testimonios tangibles, sino que se anticipan al canto y forma de otros que vendrán después, creando nuevos testimonios tangibles en plena conciencia de lo hecho hasta hoy. (Alejo Carpentier, *Los pasos perdidos*)

In the final decades of the nineteenth century lucid writers such as Manuel González Prada and José Martí opposed the fallacies of positivism (according to which some of the characteristics of the Latin race such as lack of a practical spirit, lack of discipline, impulsiveness as well as mysticism and fantasy were considered signs of inferiority) and encouraged the idea of a different America, conscious of its own values. In 1900 José Enrique Rodó published *Ariel*. His acknowledgement of the Hispanic-Greek and Latin tradition had a great influence in the future revision of the concept of the American discourse proposed by the writers of the forties on, where the ideologeme of "mestizaje" is so important.[1] During the 1940s Latin American writers were preoccupied with expressing through fiction their entire problematic reality in a way different from social realists and nativists of the preceding decade. Essayists such as Fernando Ortiz, Mariano Picón Salas, Arturo Uslar Pietri, Alfonso Reyes, and Leopoldo Zea, were concerned with revaluating and decolonizing Latin American culture, by recovering the past and acknowledging American heterogeneity.

New forms of representation seeking for a literature specific to Latin America, different from that of Europe, and breaking with old patterns are

---

[1] For a detailed study of the ideologemes of American discourse see Irlemar Chiampi's *O realismo maravilhoso* 121-73. For a relation of the cultural ideologemes to the archetypal code see Graciela N. Ricci's *Realismo mágico y conciencia mítica en América Latina* 63-87.

characteristic of the narratives of the forties and fifties. Jorge Luis Borges's *Ficciones* (1944), Miguel Angel Asturias's *El Señor Presidente* (1946), Agustín Yáñez's *Al filo del agua* (1947), Alejo Carpentier's *El reino de este mundo* (1949), Juan Carlos Onetti's *La vida breve* (1950) and Juan Rulfo's *Pedro Páramo* (1955) are some of the works which appeared during this era. Their new approach to reality will later find its prime expression in the narrative of the sixties, when formal changes already present in the two preceding decades are expanded.

Realismo maravilloso is part of the process of fictional renovation, and it aims to represent in literature the complex and varied American reality. Alejo Carpentier and Miguel Angel Asturias are recognized as the originators of this discourse in the late forties, and Gabriel García Márquez as its best example in the late sixties. However, as we shall see in the third chapter, the origins of this discourse can be traced in the writings of José de la Cuadra, in the early 1930s.

One of the characteristics of the discourse of *realismo maravilloso* is the juxtaposition of natural and supernatural elements without conflict, the intersection of myth and history to find "another sense" of reality. In this chapter I shall analyze this characteristic in order to illustrate some of the sociohistorical issues in Alejo Carpentier's *El reino de este mundo* and Gabriel García Márquez's *Cien años de soledad*.

Alejo Carpentier's *El reino de este mundo*

> La sociedad no se reconoce en el retrato que le presenta la literatura; no obstante, ese retrato fantástico es real: es el desconocido que camina a nuestro lado desde la infancia y del que no sabemos nada, salvo que es nuestra sombra (¿o somos nosotros la suya?). (Octavio Paz, *Tiempo nublado*)

In 1943 on a trip to Haiti, Alejo Carpentier had "a privileged revelation" of American reality before the ruins of Sans-Souci, the favorite residence of Henri Christophe. After this visit he wrote the famous prologue to *El reino de este mundo* on "lo real maravilloso americano" whose impact on Latin

American writers is well known.[2] In this prologue Carpentier defines the marvelous as "una iluminación inhabitual o singularmente favorecedora de las inadvertidas riquezas de la realidad" (Prólogo 9). He also talks about Latin American syncretism, its history and culture, and its different myths still alive today:

> Y es que, por la virginidad del paisaje, por la formación, por la ontología, por la presencia fáustica del indio y del negro, por la Revelación que constituyó su reciente descubrimiento, por los fecundos mestizajes que propició, América está muy lejos de haber agotado su caudal de mitologías. (Prólogo 11)

Carpentier concludes by comparing the history of America with "una crónica de lo real maravilloso." This marvelous chronicle is what he reconstructs in *El reino de este mundo*, the novel which embodies the praxis of the premises given in his prologue.

Referring to this novel Carpentier states: "el relato que va a leerse ha sido establecido sobre una documentación extremadamente rigurosa" (Prólogo 12). This is true, he incorporates not only historical documents, but also references and data from his innumerable readings and erudite knowledge. All names—except Mademoiselle Floridor—belonged to real people, and although their "historical truth" is not always exactly that which Carpentier assigns to them,[3] nevertheless, the historical incidents narrated in the novel are

---

[2]Prologue to the first edition of *El reino de este mundo* (México: EDIAPSA, 1949). This prologue was first published as an essay in the Caracas Newspaper *El Nacional* in April 8, 1948.

[3]It is known that the facts are not subjected to a strict historical rigor. Florinda Friedmann de Goldberg in her preliminary study to *El reino de este mundo* (1975, 9-44), compares the historical facts of the novel with the data given on Haiti in 1797 by the historian Moreau de Saint Méry (summarized by Alfred Métraux in *Voodoo in Haiti*). Emma Speratti-Piñero in her *Pasos hallados en "El reino de este mundo"* studies minutely the historical facts and also what is legendary, distorted, or invented by the author. Her study shows the wealth of documents consulted by Carpentier in order to write this short novel. Roberto González Echevarría in *Alejo Carpentier: The Pilgrim at Home* (103), states: "The research and the writing of *La música en Cuba* furnish Carpentier with a new working method, which consists of minute historical investigation, and creation from within a tradition that the author remakes himself with the aid of texts of different sorts." This method is evident in *El reino de este mundo*.

verifiable. Carpentier reviews events that occurred during a period of over sixty years in the history of Haiti (from Mackandal's insurrection in 1751 to the first years of Jean Pierre Boyer's government in the 1820s).

This study will not focus on the accuracy of historical facts but on the use of *realismo maravilloso* in specific moments of the three cycles presented in the novel: the description of the French colonists, Henri Christophe, and the Republican mulattoes. In all three cycles, voodoo faith, which gives the slaves hope, unity and incredible courage, is in juxtaposition to European values (presented as negative) and highlights "lo real maravilloso" of the history of Haiti. The historical facts are true but the writer uses them artistically to emphasize the myth, religion, and cultural syncretisms that culminated in the time of Henri Christophe. He succeeds in portraying the animism still alive among the followers of voodoo. This marvelous reality is an extratextual and cultural referent, and the intersections of myth with history are a constant throughout the novel (Chiampi 42).

Ti Noel, the black slave, is the linking figure in the three cycles of the novel, his master is Lenormand de Mezy, one of the French colonists. As Emil Volek rightly states:

> la perspectiva personal principal, desde la cual se proyecta la acción en el "argumento" es la del esclavo negro Ti Noel. A base de ella surge el contraste básico: los esclavos negros contra los esclavistas. En el papel de éstos se turnan diversos grupos étnicos y organizan así el contenido del "argumento" en tres cicles [sic]: el de los colonos franceses (o sea, el blanco), el de Henri Christophe (o sea, el negro) y el de los Mulatos Republicanos (sólo insinuado). El ciclo de los esclavistas comprende su ascenso y caída, pero no en todos los ciclos se expresan ambas fases explícitamente. (Volek 153)

In the first cycle, Ti Noel's recollections evoke the magical African world of Mackandal's stories when the latter was still working at the mill of Monsieur Lenormand de Mezy. The characteristic of Mackandal as great narrator and instructor is one of Carpentier's fine additions to Mackandal's legend (Friedmann 11). The contrast between the "Gran Allá" (Africa) and Europe is established by his thoughts about the kings, and African values are consistently shown to be positive:

> En el Africa, el rey era guerrero, cazador, juez y sacerdote; su simiente preciosa engrosa estirpe de héroes. En Francia, en España, en cambio, el rey enviaba sus generales a combatir; era incompetente para dirimir litigios, se hacía regañar por cualquier fraile confesor... Allá, en cambio—en Gran Allá—, había príncipes duros como el

yunque...y príncipes que mandaban sobre los cuatro puntos cardina-
les, dueños de la nube, de la semilla, del bronce y del fuego. (13)

Voodoo faith, the African marvelous world with its noble past, and the
slaves' hope in a future freedom are of capital importance. Through his
stories, Mackandal brings this world to the slaves; therefore, his disappearance
after an accident in the mill is the disappearance of that universe. When he
comes back, he is a **hungan** of the Rada rite, invested with superhuman
powers (29). As Harold Courlander explains:

> The **houngan**, priest of Vodoun . . . is a mediator, the interpreter, a
> human who has come closer to the supernatural than the others of
> his community. . . . Through the **houngan** man converses and
> communes with the forces of the universe. Through him man
> supplicates protection against impending dangers. Through him,
> sometimes a man strikes at an enemy. The **houngan** is the intellec-
> tualizing agency of a tremendous emotional force." (*Haiti Singing* 8)

This supernatural power helps Mackandal to conduct the most incredible
campaign against the whites—their death by poison—and to be feared by the
colonists. Trying to find an explanation the colonists whip and torture their
slaves, "pero el veneno seguía diezmando las familias" (28).

Mackandal is, therefore, the undefeatable revolutionary leader. The slaves
are convinced of his supernatural powers; they believe that through lycanthro-
py he will escape death (40).

After four years of metamorphoses, Mackandal is finally captured and set
on fire, but he dies only in the eyes of the white colonists, the slaves holding
a blind belief in his salvation:

> Mackandal estaba ya adosado al poste de torturas... El fuego
> comenzó a subir hacia el manco, sollamándole las piernas. En ese
> momento, Mackandal agitó su muñón que no habían podido atar, en
> un gesto conminatorio que no por menguado era menos terrible...
> Sus ataduras cayeron, y el cuerpo del negro se espigó en el aire,
> volando por sobre las cabezas, antes de hundirse en las ondas negras
> de la masa de esclavos. Un solo grito llenó la plaza.
> —**Mackandal sauvé!** (40-41)

In the above paragraph the focalization shifts constantly—from the
hangman preparing the scene, to Mackandal, and then to the slaves—and the
narrative voice provides an account of the shifts. The scene is described by an
impartial observer in the first part of the paragraph; in the second part,
Mackandal's flight is described from the perspective of the slaves.

Confusion in the crowd follows and the narrator informs the reader that
Mackandal is taken by ten soldiers and executed. The slaves who do not see
this or who refuse to believe he could die celebrate his victorious escape.
Two different cultural codes—the marvelous, that of the slaves, who have faith in
the supernatural power of voodoo, and the real, that of the colonists, who do
not understand it—are juxtaposed in this part of the narrative. A perfect
example of the marvelous of the New World where it is possible the
coexistence of the rational Western mentality as well as the "magical"
mentality of the native population. Thus, while the colonists wonder about the
insensibility of the slaves after Mackandal's death, the slaves celebrate his
triumph:

> Aquella tarde los esclavos regresaron a sus haciendas riendo por todo
> el camino. Mackandal había cumplido su promesa, permaneciendo en
> el reino de este mundo. Una vez más eran burlados los blancos por
> los Altos Poderes de la Otra Orilla... Monsieur Lenormand de Mezy,
> de gorro de dormir, comentaba con su beata esposa la insensiblidad
> de los negros ante el suplicio de un semejante. (41)

Mackandal's fame among the slaves increases with time so that he
becomes a myth, the symbol of freedom; he proves what Price-Mars calls
"l'indomptable vocation du Nègre à la jouissance de la liberté" (I.17).
Voodoo's practices as well as Mackandal's myth are still alive today:

> De Mackandal el americano...ha quedado toda una mitología,
> acompañada de himnos mágicos, conservados por todo un pueblo,
> que aún se cantan en las ceremonias de Voudou. (Prólogo 11)

Twenty years later, faith in voodoo's power is also the key factor for the
surrender of the slaves to Bouckman's influence in the ceremony at Bois
Caiman. The French Revolution affects the slaves only when Bouckman refers
to the "pacto mayor" (the solemn pact) between the slaves and the African
gods (Chiampi 43):

> El dios de los blancos ordena el crimen. Nuestros dioses nos piden
> venganza. Ellos conducirán nuestros brazos y nos darán la asistencia.
> ¡Rompan la imagen del Dios de los blancos, que tiene sed de
> nuestras lágrimas; escuchemos en nosotros mismos la llamada de la
> libertad! (52)

Carpentier's description of the Oath of Bois Caiman misses none of the
dramatic details recorded in history as it is told to school children in Haiti: the
storm, the lightning, the hymns, the Negress sacrificing a black pig and the

blood pact by which the slaves swear absolute obedience to Bouckman. Alfred Métraux in his book *Voodoo in Haiti* (95-100) records, from a *Manuel d'histoire d' Haïti*, passages on the night of August 14, 1791, when this meeting took place.

Soon after, the slaves' uprisings will begin and the colonists will be massacred in their plantations. Faith will help the slaves to accomplish incredibly courageous acts in their fight against the colonists (80).

Carpentier states in his Prologue "la sensación de lo maravilloso presupone una fe," in the novel he demonstrates how that firm belief works for the slaves, giving them unlimited confidence as well as the spirit of solidarity and determination to keep all secrets for the uprisings among themselves. There is historical data regarding the idea of invulnerability due to Ogun's protection. Métraux talks of "The power of the Loa" (95-100). James G. Leyburn in *The Haitian People* points out the importance of the **garde**, a kind of charm which people believe protects its wearer against evil of any kind. According to Leyburn, "historically the most interesting **garde** is that called a **drogue**, which is thought to insulate one against wound by weapons or bullets" (160). It is worth remembering the historical importance given by Carpentier to the Haitian Revolution which, he considers, has a profound social significance and led to national movements of independence in the continent:

> Con el juramento de Bois Caiman nace el verdadero concepto de independencia. Es decir, que al concepto de colonización traído por los españoles a Santo Domingo, en la misma tierra se une el concepto de descolonización, o sea el comienzo de las guerras de independencia, de las guerras anticoloniales que habrán de prolongarse hasta nuestros días. (qtd. in Maldonado-Denis 22)

The intersection of myth with history also occurs in the description of the last years of the French colonists, the period from the arrival of General Leclerc to his death in 1802. Of the historical figures, Giovanni Pontiero points out:

> The important contributions of prominent figures such as the colored General Rigaud and Negro Toussaint L'Ouverture are virtually ignored; Dessalines and Rochambeau are mentioned only briefly; Leclerc remains a somewhat shadowy figure by comparison with his wife. (Pontiero 530)

Carpentier concentrates on Paulina Bonaparte and also portrays in detail a fictional character, Solimán. Through them emerges the obvious juxtaposition of the real-Europe and marvelous-Haiti.

On the island of La Tortue where Paulina lives surrounded by luxury, her frivolous attitude contrasts with that of the troubled and preoccupied Leclerc. While her husband worries about the slaves' insurrections and the increasing problems for the colonists, she indulges in a life of pleasure. She hires a black servant, Solimán, to care for her body and whom, she knew, was continually tortured by desire (73). Her erotic fancy comes to an end when yellow fever decimates the region, and Leclerc is one of the victims. A terrified Paulina turns to Solimán and surrenders completely to his mysterious rites—voodoo—which appeal to her more than "las mentiras del Directorio, en cuyo descreimiento había cobrado conciencia de existir" (76). Ironically, voodoo awakes in her the practices of her Corsican childhood. Here Solimán, who has been acting mainly as a servant, reveals another aspect of his personality: he appears as **hungan** performing a rite on Paulina (77). This rite, as Speratti-Piñero argues, seems to be the rite of Petro Loa where Legba is one of the loa. According to Métraux:

> A **hungan** may advise his patient to have recourse to the **petro** and to submit to rites which, however frightening, can bring about an immediate cure...But the price they claim for their favors is high: any transaction with the **petro loa** entails risk. (Métraux 89)

Solimán took this risk by putting Paulina, a white who was not initiated in voodoo, under the protection of the loa and he will be punished for this act.

After Leclerc's death Paulina leaves the island with an amulet to Papá Legba, wrought by Solimán. The amulet protects Paulina from danger in America. After her departure, the rest of the colonists, under the government of Rochambeau, start a life of orgies (78).

Solimán reappears in the narrative as Henri Christophe's valet, helping him during his sickness (109), then accompanying the King's family to bury his corpse at La Ferrière (117-119), and finally in Italy as servant to Christophe's exiled family (125-136). Here he will be punished for his past actions, when one night while visiting his lover—a servant of the Borghese Palace—he encounters the Venus of Canova and remembers the past. The statue becomes for him Paulina on the island La Tortue, and Legba punishes him for his previous errors.

> Aquel viaje de las manos le refrescó la memoria trayendo imágenes de muy lejos. El había conocido en otros tiempos aquel contacto... Y, de pronto, movido por una imperiosa rememoración física, Solimán comenzó a hacer los gestos del masajista... Pero, súbitamente, la frialdad del mármol subida a sus muñecas con tenazas de muerte, lo inmovilizó en un grito". (129-30)

Solimán becomes frantic; when the gendarmes arrive, he escapes through
a window. Victim of the malaria fever, not even Dr. Antommarchi—Napole-
on's doctor on St. Helena—can cure him, for he keeps calling "Papá Legba,
para que le abriese los caminos del regreso a Santo Domingo" (131).
Solimán regrets his betrayal and asks for pardon. He has not only
betrayed the voodoo by taking sides with those who do not practice it, but in
Europe he has been denying his past. The narrative is left open in this part;
thus the reader does not know whether or not Solimán receives forgiveness
from Legba.

Contrary to the open-endedness of Solimán's destiny is that of Henri
Christophe, whose portrayal dominates the novel. In his story it is possible to
follow the fate of those who betray voodoo. The historical figure of Henri
Christophe is in itself contradictory, full of negative and positive anecdotes,
according to the passions or interests of people and interpreted by historians
in different ways. Different interpretations are given by Ardouin, Bonnet,
Placide-Justin, Mackenzie, Schatz, and others.[4] Carpentier uses the most
convenient interpretation for his purpose; his characterization of the monarch
favors mythical beliefs and is directly related to the voodoo faith.
Christophe's life is, as Carpentier states:

> una historia imposible de situar en Europa, y que es tan real, sin
> embargo, como cualquier suceso ejemplar de los consignados, para
> pedagógica edificación, en los manuales escolares. (Prólogo 12)

A former master chef, he then becomes a soldier of the colonial artillery
fighting for Haiti's independence by supporting Jean-Jacques Dessalines. After
Dessalines's death he is elected president in 1805, but he is opposed by the
Senate. Christophe goes to "Llanura del Norte" and proclaims himself
emperor, establishing his domain while imitating the Napoleonic courtly style.
He builds the magnificent palace of Sans-Souci and the colossal fortress of La
Ferrière, where he imposes a slavery worse than that of the colonists. After
the rebellion of his people, he kills himself; the fortress that was intended to
protect him against his enemies becomes his tomb.

Although the novel's focus is on the period of Christophe's kingdom to his
fall and death, the reader also learns briefly about his former days as master
chef and later as owner of the "Albergue de La Corona" in the Cap (45-46),
and of his time as a soldier of the colonial artillery (62).

---

[4]For information on this subject consult the bibliography given by Speratti-
Piñero 202-12.

The discovery of his marvelous kingdom is made by Ti Noel who, now an old but free man, thanks God to be back in his native Haiti, "the land of the Great Pacts." Like the rest of the slaves, he is convinced of the supernatural power of voodoo which made possible the triumph of Dessalines:

> Porque él sabía—y lo sabían todos los negros franceses de Santiago de Cuba—que el triunfo de Dessalines se debía a una preparación tremenda, en la que habían intervenido Loco, Petro, Ogún, Ferraille, Bruse-Pimba, Caplou-Pimba, Marinette Bois-Cheche y todas las divinidades de la pólvora y del fuego. (85)

Ti Noel's belief in the power of the African gods molds his understanding of the happenings in Henri Christophe's kingdom.

While walking to the old plantation of Lenormand de Mezy, he encounters black officers in Napoleonic garb. Fascinated, he follows them, only to marvel before geometrical gardens, columns, cupolas, terraces, pergolas, artificial brooks, statues, arcades; and a pink palace with oval windows where ladies are visible, wearing plumed headdresses. He has arrived at Henri Christophe's kingdom where everybody is black:

> Pero lo que más asombraba a Ti Noel era el descubrimiento de que ese mundo prodigioso, como no lo habían conocido los gobernadores franceses del Cabo, era un mundo de negros. (89)

In the description of Ti Noel arriving at Sans-Souci the perception of the marvelous works at different levels, and the modulation of the narrative voice provides an account of them; the comparisons between Europe and America are from the perspective of a cultured narrator. However, Ti Noel's point of view is also expressed: his amazement at the vision of Negroes not only as slaves (with which he was familiar), but also as masters, a position that, in his experience, was only for white people.

On a trip to Cap, after the death of Monsieur Lenormand de Mezy's second wife, Ti Noel had witnessed the success of chef Henri Christophe, former cook and then owner of La Corona (45-46). At that time Ti Noel was still a young man. Now, in his old age, he is contemplating the luxury of the court at Sans-Souci, but a heavy blow across his back awakens him, to his amazement. He experiences terrible sufferings at the fortress of La Ferrière where slavery is worse than the one at the time of the French colonists:

> puesto que había una infinita miseria en lo de verse apaleado por un negro, tan negro como uno... Era como si en una misma casa los hijos pegaran a los padres, el nieto a la abuela, las nueras a la madre que cocinaba. (95-96)

After serving at La Ferrière, Ti Noel hears the horrifying howls of Corneille Breille, previous confessor of Henri Christophe, condemned by him to die in the Archbishop's Palace (101); finally, he participates in the pillage of Sans-Souci after Christophe's death (133).

Convinced of the power of the loa, Ti Noel and the black people believe that Christophe's fall is the god's punishment for his betrayal of voodoo. Christophe made a big mistake in constructing La Ferrière:

> La sangre de toros que habían bebido aquellas paredes tan espesas era de recurso infalible contra las armas de blancos. Pero esa sangre jamás había sido dirigida contra los negros... Christophe, el reformador, había querido ignorar el vodú. (114)

Henri Christophe betrayed his people, but first of all he offended the voodoo deities by adopting the Catholic faith; thus the rites at La Ferrière where he had implanted slavery could not help him. In this novel Carpentier portrays the animism predominant in the African cultures which he regretted not having done in his first novel *Ecue-Yamba-O*.[5]

Christophe's punishment starts on August 15 during the mass. Despite all the arrangements, the King feels a hostile atmosphere. From far off he hears the beat of drums. Then, suddenly at the Offertory, before the altar arises the figure of Corneille Breille, the immured priest who was "intoning the Dies Irae." At that moment, a thunderbolt strikes Christophe to the floor leaving him paralyzed (107).

Christophe's fit of apoplexy is a historical fact, which happened on August 15, 1820. González Echevarría quotes Charles Moran's description of this incident:

> One Sunday, a few weeks later [after the execution of Brelle (sic); the footnote indicates here that "August 15 is the date usually given"], the king suddenly presented himself at the little parish church at Limonade and sent word to the priest that he desired to hear mass. The astonished curate made ready, but as he entered the chancel he was horrified to see the king rise, clutching his prie-Dieu, mutter the name of Corneille Brelle and fall forward in faint, opening a deep gash in his forehead as it struck the pavement. (*The Pilgrim at Home* 138)

There is a legend regarding Corneille Breille's death in which not only archbishop González but the same Christophe were involved. The 15th of

---

[5]See C. Leante's "Confesiones sencillas" 22.

August is also an important date in Catholicism, the Assumption of the Virgin. Carpentier uses that date for the rising of Corneille Breille and the thunderbolt, for in Voodoo faith Shango is the deity of Lightning who protects his followers but also punishes those who offend him. Thus, the amalgamation of history and legend provided Carpentier with rich material for the tragic punishment of the black king describing it with the Caribbean voodoo, the syncretism of Christian and African practices. Carpentier skillfully makes use, in the narrative, of all voodoo's nuances. It might help to review Courlander's explanation of voodoo:

> Vodoun is conservative, that it is a repository of old beliefs, that it has an internal dynamic, and that it is a system of organization of known and unknown forces. If it has had more meaning to most Haitians than Christian doctrine, it is because Christianity has seemed to offer only doctrine and guidelines to behavior, whereas Vodoun offers doctrine, social controls, a pattern of family relations, direct communication with original forces, emotional release, dance, music, meaningful socializing, drama, theater, legend and folklore, motivation, alternatives to threatening dangers, individual initiatives through placation and invocation, treatment of ailments by means of herb lotions and rituals, protection of fields, fertility, and a continuing familiar relationship with the ancestors. ("Vodoun in Haitian Culture" 21)

During the insurrection of his people Henri Christophe experiences his worst days. He remains dramatically alone, abandoned and betrayed by his people during a dark night penetrated by the sound of drums (113). Christophe understands his mistake, "había querido ignorar el vodú, formando, a fustazos, una casta de señores católicos" (114). He ends his life dressed in his "richest ceremonial attire" while the pounding of the drums gets closer (115).

By betraying the voodoo, Christophe also betrays his past. Forgetting the greatness and courage of the African kings, who were "true kings," he establishes his kingdom by imitating those of Europe, exploiting his fellow-men and reducing them to a slavery "worse than the other." Christophe offended the gods of Lightning and the gods of Thunder, thus he had to be punished.

In Christophe's kingdom, not only the luxury of the court that surpasses that of Europe but also the horrors at La Ferrière are marvelous. Carpentier utilizes a surrealistic concept of marvelous which he learned during his years in Paris in the late twenties. Although in his Prologue Carpentier attacked the artificiality of surrealistic methods to create the marvelous, some years later he acknowledged the importance of surrealism in his work:

El surrealismo sí significó mucho para mí. Me enseñó a ver texturas, aspectos de la vida americana que no había advertido, envueltos como estábamos en la ola de nativismo traída por Güiraldes, Gallegos y José Eustasio Rivera. Comprendí que detrás de ese nativismo había algo más; lo que llamo los contextos: contexto telúrico y contexto épico-político: el que halle la relación entre ambos escribirá la novela americana. (qtd. in Leante 21-22)

Carpentier's marvelous reveals the "other sense" of reality, hence going beyond the ludic. It aims to portray Haiti's different contexts as well as to criticize oppression of all kinds and to highlight men's rebellious spirit and fight for freedom.

In the cycle of the Republican Mulattoes, Ti Noel continues the task initiated by Mackandal and Bouckman, and he too becomes a mythical figure. In "his kingdom"—the old house of Lenormand de Mezy—Ti Noel has his "treasures" retrieved from the pillage of the Palace of Sans-Souci. Since he has been possessed by the spirit of the King of Angola, he now issues orders to the wind (135). The King of Angola is one of the loas; once he is possessed by this loa Ti Noel comes in contact with immortality because as Courlander explains, "Once a man becomes possessed of a loa he is marked. Already, while he lives, he has come into intimate contact with immortality. And when he dies possibly he will go to live in the 'island below the sea', and becomes in his turn a loa" (*Haiti Singing* 15). This act as will be seen later helps to explain the resolution of the novel.

Ti Noel's power does not last long, for new masters, the Republican Mulattoes, come to the region, and the slavery situation returns. Tired by "ese inacabable retoñar de cadenas," Ti Noel decides to escape by imitating Mackandal's metamorphosis. His fate, however, is not better than when he is a man and he goes through several metamorphoses.

Ti Noel transforms himself from a bird into a wasp and then into an ant. In this last state he has to perform tasks that "demasiado le recordaban los mayorales de Lenorman de Mezy, los guardias de Christophe, los mulatos de ahora" (139-140). Then, he takes the form of a goose thinking that "los gansos eran gente de orden, de fundamento y de sistema" (142) but he is rejected because "se presentaba, sin el menor expediente de limpieza de sangre" (143). In other words, he had no past. At this time he understands his error; "Mackandal se había disfrazado de animal, durante años, para servir a los hombres, no para desertar del terreno de los hombres" (143). Thus, recovering his human form, he accepts his task and feels his sense of responsibility as a man. Acknowledging his African forebears, he tries to vindicate himself. Climbing upon his table:

lanzó su declaración de guerra a los nuevos amos, dando orden a sus
súbditos de partir al asalto de las obras insolentes de los mulatos.
(144)

Like Mackandal and Bouckman, Ti Noel leads the rebellion against the
oppressors. After his war declaration "a great green wind" blows:

Y desde aquella hora nadie supo más de Ti Noel... salvo, tal vez,
aquel buitre mojado...que acabó por plegarse y hundir el vuelo en las
espesuras de Bois Caimán. (144-45)

In this last part of the novel Ti Noel has been associated with Christ.
Friedmann interprets Ti Noel as a kind of Christ, symbolizing humanity (22-
24, 36, 41, 44). González Echevarría holds a similar view; for him Ti Noel is
"a sort of figura Christi" (144). There are homologies to Biblical passages,
perhaps one of the most telling is when women saw Ti Noel they waved cloths
in sign of reverence (135).

Ti Noel stays, fulfilling his mission among mankind. As Carpentier once
said, "*El reino de este mundo* se titula así porque es una inversión del reino
de los cielos de los teólogos" (qtd. in Roa 30). This usage of Biblical passages
to serve specific purposes in the diegesis[6] is one of the characteristics of the
writers of marvelous realism. I shall address again the topic with García
Márquez, Aguilera Malta, and Yánez Cossío who also use Biblical passages
and different cultural sources to express the distinctive characteristics of the
cultural mix of the Americas, where, according to Carpentier, "todavía no se
ha terminado de establecer, por ejemplo, un recuento de cosgomonías"
(Prólogo 10).

Carpentier portrays the concept of animism in the Haitian people and as
it will be observed in the fourth chapter, animism also exists in other parts of
Latin America; Aguilera Malta portrays it in the Ecuadorian blacks and Yánez
Cossío in the Indians of the Andean region. Considering Carpentier's interest
in highlighting voodoo's animism in the Caribbean culture I hold that the most
accurate interpretation of the conclusion of the novel is that of Speratti-
Piñero's. She posits that this last page is an apotheosis of Ti Noel. Before
dying, convinced that his mission can be performed only in this world, he
transforms himself into a vulture and flies to the Bois Caiman, the place
where Bouckman talked about freedom in 1791.

---

[6]Term adopted by Gérard Genette from the theoreticians of cinemato-
graphic narrative. It has the same meaning of "stoire" or narrative content. See
his *Narrative Discourse* 27.

To support this theory one has to consider that, according to Voodoo, a man who has been possessed by a loa can also be converted into a loa. Due to his contact with immortality, and helped by the loa, he adopts an animal form. Thus converted into a new loa, he can even come back to live on earth. We learn that "llevado a un toque de tambores, Ti Noel había caído en posesión del rey de Angola" (135); therefore, this last transformation is possible. As the vulture who flies to Bois Caiman, like Mackandal and Bouckman, he becomes a myth.

In all the sequences which we have analyzed, there is a constant intersection of myth with history. All of the slaves' revolts reveal how Carpentier used voodoo and its followers' faith in its supernatural powers as the revolutionary moving force. The juxtaposition of Europe and America presented in the first chapter is maintained throughout the novel; its correlative is the juxtaposition of oppression and freedom. Freedom is always positively expressed, and oppression is consistently condemned. Henri Christophe fails because he imitated European values and tried to impose on his fellow men the same slavery he had opposed. Oppression repeats itself cyclically and man rebels against his oppressor systematically. Ti Noel's last revolutionary message extols continuous revolt against oppression of any kind; he remains in the "kingdom of this world" where "la grandeza del hombre está precisamente en querer mejorar lo que es" (144). Like *realismo maravilloso* itself, Carpentier's narrative draws from the astounding variety of cultural expression and its metamorphoses in the Caribbean. A founding narrative of *realismo maravilloso*, *El reino de este mundo* is a key novel of what will follow in this tradition.

Gabriel García Márquez's *Cien años de soledad*

> En ese instante gigantesco, he visto millones de actos deleitables o atroces; ninguno me asombró como el hecho de que todos ocuparan el mismo punto, sin superposición y sin transparencia. (Jorge Luis Borges, *El aleph*)

The decade of the 1960s is of capital importance in Latin American narrative. The renovation of the novel already started by some of the writers of the 1930s, through the 1950s now takes on a definite force and gives a completely new structure to the Latin American novel. New forms of representation aiming to draw a multivalent image of reality, a complex linguistic structure, and a broad variety of subjects and forms resulted in the emergence of novels that attracted international attention. Some of those novels are: Augusto Roa Bastos's *Hijo de Hombre* (1960), Juan Carlos Onetti's *El astillero* (1961), Ernesto Sábato's *Sobre héroes y tumbas* (1961), Alejo Carpentier's *El siglo de las luces* (1962), Carlos Fuentes's *La muerte de Artemio Cruz* (1962), Mario Vargas Llosa's *La ciudad y los perros* (1962), Julio Cortázar's *Rayuela* (1963), Guillermo Cabrera Infante's *Tres tristes tigres* (1964), José Lezama Lima's *Paradiso* (1966), Gabriel García Márquez's *Cien años de soledad* (1967), Severo Sarduy's *De dónde son los cantantes* (1967), Salvador Helizondo's *El hipogeo secreto* (1968), and Manuel Puig's *La traición de Rita Hayworth* (1968). From the seventies on, the number and variety of novels are so rich that it is not possible to restrict the writings to a categorical listing.

The discourse of *realismo maravilloso* during this time has as its main axis the questioning of language. There is also an inquiry into the nature of reality and a continuous call for the participation of the reader. The relationship between narrator, narratee and cultural context is essential. Complex Latin American realities are presented through the juxtaposition of real and marvelous semantic categories, described by Greimas as "isotopie."[7] Thus *realismo maravilloso* with its origins in the early 1930s now becomes definitely a new way of writing. Many social, historical, political and ideological issues are treated through the questioning of the enunciation and the use of imagination, and by breaking the barriers of time and space. Gabriel García Márquez is considered the leader of this new way of writing. His novel, *Cien años de soledad*, exemplifies both the problems and triumphs of this mode of writing.

Towards the end of *Cien años de soledad*, Aureliano realizes that the final protection of the encoded history of the family written by Melquíades was that he had concentrated "a century of daily episodes in such a way that they coexisted in one instant." In this way, Melquíades protected the manuscripts from reductionism, thus the century of daily episodes that constitutes the book allows such a plurality of readings that makes it impossible to reduce the text to any one specific problem.

The readings vary and could be multiplied by the number of readers. According to Rodríguez Monegal, "The simultaneity of readings reinforces the concept of the world as a book" ("The Last Three Pages" 488). For Carlos Fuentes it is "una historia del origen y destino del tiempo humano y de los

---

[7]Greimas in "Élements pour une théorie de l'interpretation du récit mythique," defines narrative isotopie as the "ensemble redondant de catégories sémantiques qui rend possible la lecture uniforme du récit, telle qu'elle résulte des lectures partielles des énonces après résolution de leurs ambiguïtés, cette résolution elle même étant guidée par la recherche de la lecture unique." *Communications* 8 (1966): 30. I use this term in my analysis.

sueños y deseos con lo que los hombres se conservan o destruyen" (qtd. in Vargas Llosa, *Historia de un deicidio* 78). Ariel Dorfman states that the novel "permite la construcción de una metáfora gigantesca en que se cifra toda la historia del continente americano" (*Imaginación y violencia en América* 139). Agustín Cueva considers that the novel "puede ser leída como metáfora histórica del subdesarrollo" ("Para una interpretación sociológica" 15). For Tzvetan Todorov "se trata de una epopeya moderna: escrita en la época de la novela, y 'corrupta' por ella" ("Macondo en París" 44). The list could continue.

The juxtaposition of real and marvelous isotopies without conflict and the nondisjunction of contradictory terms is the main characteristic of the discourse of *realismo maravilloso*. In *Cien años de soledad* this juxtaposition is a constant. At the risk of falling into the reader's trap of reducing the novel, it is nonetheless worthwhile to provide a brief general summary of the story in order to pursue our analysis. We can say that *Cien años de soledad* is the chronicle of one hundred years in the life of seven generations of Buendías. Characters break the barriers of time and space, interacting among generations during life and after death, in a world where the unusual is the norm and where repetition of names, circumstances, facts, people is a constant. Macondo is a young community established by José Arcadio Buendía and his wife Ursula Iguarán, together with a group of friends. The reader learns the whole cycle of its existence, from its foundation to its destruction. It starts as a fresh world "el mundo era tan reciente, que muchas cosas carecían de nombre" (9), it is an ideal place "donde nadie era mayor de treinta años y donde nadie había muerto" (16). Before establishing Macondo the founding couple, who are cousins, lived in Riohacha, they left because José Arcadio Buendía killed Prudencio Aquilar. Ursula lives haunted by fear of a curse on incest. (An aunt of Ursula married a cousin and they had a son with a pig's tail). In this first stage, Macondo is a patriarchal society with its own laws and without exterior problematic interferences. The central figure is José Arcadio Buendía, a man of extraordinary imagination, indefatigable in his search for knowledge. He becomes mad and is tied to a chestnut tree.

In its second phase, the arcadian existence of Macondo is disrupted by governmental and religious authorities coming from the exterior world. Once politics is part of the development of the city, life becomes complex. There is a long period of violence; the innumerable uprisings are led by Colonel Aureliano Buendía (second son of José Arcadio Buendía) who becomes a mythical revolutionary figure, and finally gets lost "en la soledad de su inmenso poder" (146).

The third stage of Macondo comes with the establishment of the banana company. The twins José Arcadio Segundo and Aureliano Segundo, great-grandchildren of the founder of the family, play an important role. At the beginning there is a period of abundance symbolized by Aureliano Segundo's prosperity and by his concubine Petra Cotes, "cuyo amor tenía la virtud de exasperar a la naturaleza" (166). On the other hand, there is a reemergence of violence with the addition of exploitation. When the banana company finally leaves, Macondo is almost in ruins.

The novel concludes with the fulfillment of the curse on the family after Amaranta Ursula and Aureliano Babilonia (children of the fifth and sixth generations respectively) consummate the feared incest. Amaranta Ursula dies after giving birth to a son with a pig's tail. Finally, while "all the ants in the world" drag the last Aureliano toward their holes, Aureliano Babilonia understands Melquíades's epigraph: "El primero de la estirpe está amarrado en un árbol y al último se lo están comiendo las hormigas" (349). Thus he finishes deciphering the manuscripts and learns his destiny; simultaneous to his reading, "a biblical hurricane" destroys the city. Being aware of the richness of the text and taking into consideration the impossibility of reducing the novel to one single problem, I shall not attempt a global interpretation. Rather, I shall analyze three specific moments in the narrative which allow three types of rationalistic discourse through the use of *realismo maravilloso*: the Buendías's visit to see the ice; the rise to heaven of Remedios the Beauty; and the arrival of the banana company in Macondo. In each one of these moments the juxtaposition of marvelous and real isotopies convey different systems of belief.

According to García Márquez, the scene of the ice was the first image he had for the novel. It was a memory from his childhood when he went to the circus with his grandfather. Thus he described it as a circus novelty (Vargas Llosa, *Historia de un deicidio* 46).

When gypsies come to town, José Arcadio Buendía takes his sons José Arcadio and Aureliano to the circus to see the invention of the "sages of Memphis." The ice is presented as a spectacle to be admired. Every detail in the description is meant to build expectation. It is announced as an extraordinary invention; it is exhibited in a tent of the 10th century B.C., and it is kept in a "pirate chest" watched by "a giant." When the chest is opened, the ice gives off "a glacial exhalation."

> Al ser destapado por el gigante, el cofre dejó escapar un aliento glacial. Dentro sólo había un enorme bloque transparente, con infinitas agujas internas...José Arcadio Buendía se atrevió a murmurar:
> —Es el diamante más grande del mundo.
> —No —corrigió el gitano—. Es hielo. (22-23)

Without understanding, José Arcadio Buendía wants to touch it, but first he has to pay for the privilege. When he touches it, his sensation is extraordinary:

"el corazón se le hinchaba de temor y júbilo al contacto del misterio" (23); thus he pays again to repeat his experience.

The narrator presents as marvelous an advance in technology, common in any developed place. However, for the inhabitants of Macondo it is a mystery, a novelty; José Arcadio's reaction of fear and jubilation is logical, as is also his admiration for such an invention. As Josefina Ludmer rightly states: "La escena del hielo...funciona como eje inicial de la temporalidad, como instauración del 'código de las maravillas' (de la irrealidad, de la ficción)" (Ludmer, *Cien años* 53).

When the gypsies bring the ice, Macondo is in its first stage. Thus occurs the opposition between man in close contact with nature and science, which comes from the outside world. Referring to this scene of the ice, Fernando Alegría remarks:

> Los hechos son inmediatos y concretos: es un niño quien va a conocer el hielo de la mano de su padre; pero la imagen resultante, desprovista de límites temporales, trasciende la ocasión y recrea el pasado de la humanidad. (*Nueva historia* 315)

Like the ice, technological discoveries such as the magnet, the telescope, the magnifying glass, and the false teeth of Melquíades are described as extraordinary. The reader accepts the amazed reaction of the characters before such objects because these characters logically perceive them in accordance with their world view. This kind of presentation of the natural as extraordinary is common in the different stages of Macondo, which is always behind with respect to the development of the outside world. When Macondo starts its industrial stage, any modern development (the train, electricity, the cinema, the telephone) causes a similar reaction of amazement.

The opposite technique to the supernaturalization of the ordinary is used when extraordinary facts are presented as natural. Supernatural things are accepted without bewilderment by the characters as well as by the reader. This reality does not produce an effect of amazement but of enchantment. There are many of these instances in *Cien años*. The rise to heaven of Remedios the Beauty, for example, is done within the limits of a realistic representation.

Remedios the Beauty is José Arcadio Buendía's great-granddaughter. She is described as different from the rest of the family. She is "la única que permaneció inmune a la peste del banano" (199), she ignores the impression her beauty caused among men (200). It is established that she is not a common type of character, for she neither keeps fixed schedules nor conforms to general rules (204). However, like any of the other women, when she is around, she participates in the activities of the house. One day when all the

women were helping Fernanda to fold some sheets Amaranta noticed that
Remedios the Beauty was extremely pale:

> —¿Te sientes mal? —le preguntó.
> Remedios, la bella, que tenía agarrada la sábana por el otro extremo,
> hizo una sonrisa de lástima.
> —Al contrario, —dijo—, nunca me he sentido mejor.
> Acabó de decirlo, cuando Fernanda sintió que un delicado viento de
> luz le arrancó las sábanas de las manos... Amaranta...trató de
> agarrarse de la sábana para no caer, en el instante en que Remedios,
> la bella, empezaba a elevarse. (204)

In this passage the supernatural event is introduced as a natural physical
effect on the appearance of Remedios, making a logically impossible action
seem completely plausible. The situation is presented as if Remedios's intense
paleness were the logical antecedent for what comes next, her rise into
heaven. To obtain this effect, the narrative voice accounts for the realistic and
marvelous planes without antinomy. The assertive tone of the narration
contributes to make "real" the "marvelous." There are no terms that indicate
any hesitation or allude to the unusual.

While the marvelous is never questioned by the inhabitants of Macondo
who believed in the miracle, the foreigners do not believe. Without judging the
facts, the narrator simply states what happens. Thus, the reader learns of the
skepticism of the foreigners and Fernanda's prayers to recover her sheets:

> Los forasteros, por supuesto, pensaron que Remedios, la bella, había
> sucumbido por fin a su irrevocable destino de abeja reina, y que su
> familia trataba de salvar la honra con la patraña de la levitación.
> Fernanda, mordida por la envidia, terminó por aceptar el prodigio,
> y durante mucho tiempo siguió rogando a Dios que le devolviera las
> sábanas. (205)

Referring to this episode, García Márquez gives a simple explanation. He
asserts that there was indeed a beautiful girl like Remedios, who escaped with
a man, and that her family, to avoid embarrassment, invented the story of her
rise to heaven together with the sheets (*Diálogo* 19).

It is known that writers of *realismo maravilloso* utilize Biblical passages
in a special way, reversing traditional interpretations to serve specific purposes
in the diegesis. There are several instances in *Cien años* when this happens,
one of the most noticeable perhaps, being the reversal of the Cain and Abel
passage in the story of the seventeen Aurelianos. In Genesis 4:15 one reads,
"And the LORD said unto him, Therefore whosoever slayeth Cain, vengeance
shall be taken on him sevenfold. And the LORD set a mark upon Cain, lest

any finding him should kill him." As we know, the mark put on the seventeen Aurelianos was not to prevent their death but to assure it.[8]

In the rise to heaven of Remedios the Beauty, however, there is not a reversal of any Biblical passage, and one can read the scene as an homology to the dogma of the Assumption of the Virgin Mary. This passage then could correspond to what Jung calls a "psychic" truth: "Physical is not the only criterion of truth: there are also psychic truths which can neither be explained nor proved nor contested in any physical way" (*Answer to Job* xi).[9]

Carl G. Jung examines the psychological background of the dogma and considers that it is:

> the most important religious event since the Reformation. . . . It does not matter at all that a physically impossible fact is asserted, because all religious assertions are physical impossibilities. . . . [R]eligious statements without exception have to do with the reality of the **psyche** and not with the reality of **physis**. (*Answer to Job* 102)

Regarding Protestant reaction he adds:

---

[8]In her study of *Cien años de soledad*, Josefina Ludmer analyzes this scene explaining the reversal of the Biblical passage and all the variations:

> No es Caín, el que mató a su hermano **menor** Abel, a quien se pone la señal, sino a los hijos de Aureliano (que no mató a su hermano **mayor** José Arcadio, o por lo menos no se indica directamente que lo haya matado, sino a un hermano figurado, opuesto político y militar, Moncada); las señales no se ponen para no ser matados sino para serlo; las siete veces del eventual castigo se transforman en diecisiete (el número de los hijos de Aureliano a quienes grabó la cruz). Este juego con el dato bíblico tiene todos los rasgos de la **parodia**. (128-29)

[9]In 1950 Pope Pius XII established the dogma of the bodily assumption of Mary into heaven. He wrote in his Apostolic Constitution *Munificentissimus Deus* that Mary was assumed into heaven "and, like her Son before her, to conquer death and to be raised body and soul to the glory of heaven, to shine refulgent as Queen at the right hand of her Son, the immortal King of ages." (McBrien, *Catholicism* 2:881). Nothing is said about the manner or time of her assumption. According to McBrien, Protestant reaction to this dogma was negative, but for Catholics, after the disasters of the first and second world wars, the dogma came at "an appropriate moment to reaffirm the dignity of the human body and to rekindle faith in the resurrection of the body" (McBrien 881).

The logical consistency of the papal declaration cannot be surpassed, and it leaves Protestantism with the odium of being nothing but a man's religion which allows no metaphysical representation of woman. (*Answer to Job* 102, 103)

The dogma then is accepted as a spiritual need and also as a revalorization of women. We can consider that since there are no details regarding the manner of the assumption in the rise to heaven of Remedios the Beauty, there is no reversal in the facts, as in the scene of the seventeen Aurelianos. The "assumption" of Remedios the Beauty does not need a reversal, for it is not based on a Biblical passage, but it is an homology to people's faith. In the Assumption of the Virgin, according to Jung, the collective unconscious was at work (99). In Remedios the Beauty's passage there is at work the collective unconscious of the inhabitants of Macondo who believed in the miracle (205). The narrative voice gives account of both the Catholic tradition—what the inhabitants of Macondo believe—and the Protestants' reaction—the foreigners, who do not believe. There is no reversal of Remedios's characterization, for she is innocent, a virgin, and different from the rest of the Buendías; she too was "preserved" from sin, in this case the sin of incest which is common to the Buendías. This scene is a representation of a traditional belief which is accepted as part of the cultural heritage. The portrayal of both points of view in this scene is similar to what we observed in Mackandal's flight in *El reino de este mundo* where the narrator presented two points of view: that of the slaves and that of the French colonists. The slaves' perception was also based on a popular belief.

Who is telling the truth? is the question posed to the reader through the juxtaposition of marvelous and natural elements in the massacre of the banana workers where the "official story" is opposed to the popular version. Historical facts are described in the same hyperbolic terms as are the other facts of the novel, but the reality of the violence and exploitation is exposed in the text, calling for the pact between the narrator and the reader to interpret the "other sense." Thus the reader is forced to reflect on the issues presented and starts questioning historical facts, and finds that many times reality surpasses the amazement of the imaginary. To this particular García Márquez states:

Yo nací y crecí en el Caribe. Lo conozco país por país, isla por isla, y tal vez de allí provenga mi frustración de que nunca se me ha ocurrido nada ni he podido hacer nada que sea más asombroso que la realidad. Lo más lejos que he podido llegar es a trasponerla con recursos políticos, pero no hay una sola línea en ninguno de mis libros que no tenga su origen en un hecho real. ("Fantasía y creación" 7)

This is the serious enchantment of *realismo maravilloso* which goes beyond the ludic and which can illuminate social problems effectively. For, as Bakhtin says in *The Dialogic Imagination*, "the prose writer makes use of words that are already populated with the social intentions of others and compels them to serve his own new intentions, to serve a second master" (299-300).

Historical facts are presented as purely imaginative; the uninformed reader can take them to be part of the fictitious plot. However, if Colonel Aureliano Buendia's revolutions are a correlative to Colombia's years of violence with the banana company, as Cueva rightly states, the problematization of the novel develops another level. It becomes a "dilatada metáfora de la explotación y la violencia en América Latina" ("Para una interpretación sociológica" 13). The banana problem is introduced as one more of the plagues that destroy Macondo. The treatment of the natural and the political as extraordinary works in the narrative at different levels.

A banana, an ordinary thing for the inhabitants of Macondo, is treated by a foreigner as something extraordinary. This scene is homologous to that of the ice at the beginning of the novel. The ice's description as marvelous is parallel to Mr. Herbert's treatment of the banana. If at the beginning the ice was presented as if it were a precious thing, now the detailed examination of the fruit as well as that of the atmosphere, the measure of the temperature, the level of humidity, and the intensity of the light, is also extraordinary. The inhabitants of Macondo experience the atmospheric fluctuations and changes in nature which were considered reserved for God now being done by foreign engineers, agronomists, hydrologists, and topographers brought by Mr. Herbert:

> Dotados de recursos que en otra época estuvieron reservados a la Divina Providencia, modificaron el régimen de lluvias, apresuraron el ciclo de las cosechas, y quitaron el río de donde estuvo siempre y lo pusieron...detrás del cementerio. Fue en esa ocasión cuando construyeron una fortaleza de hormigón sobre la descolorida tumba de José Arcadio, para que el olor a pólvora del cadáver no contaminara las aguas. (197)

The marvelous element of the smell of powder of José Arcadio Segundo's corpse is juxtaposed to the reality of the exploitation of the region by the foreign company. In the above quotation the last phrase reinforces the marvelous. Historical facts are consistently introduced in the narrative by juxtaposing marvelous and real elements. In relating the changes introduced in Macondo by the banana company, García Márquez works directly with

historical documents from Colombia's Magdalena region during 1928 when the
United Fruit Company was there.[10]

Historical and social changes are exposed in a dialectical way; nothing is
missing; foreign interference transforms everything, and the reign of violence
begins:

> Cuando llegó la compañía bananera...los funcionarios locales fueron
> sustituídos por forasteros autoritarios... Los antiguos policías fueron
> reemplazados por sicarios de machetes. (206)

There is social discrimination by the foreigners toward the inhabitants of
Macondo:

> Los gringos...hicieron un pueblo aparte al otro lado de la línea del
> tren... El sector estaba cercado por una malla metálica, como un
> gigantesco gallinero electrificado... (197)

Social discrimination in the inhabitants of Macondo is symbolized by the
attitude of Fernanda, Aureliano Segundo's wife, for whom: "la gente de bien
era la que no tenía nada que ver con la compañía bananera" (217).

This exposition of similar reactions in both groups is different from and
more effective than the Manicheanism of the social realism of the thirties and
is characteristic of the writers of new realism. The plague of the banana
company is treated as the other plagues (the insomnia, the oblivion, the war)
that destroy Macondo. The narrator continues introducing historical facts
through the fragmentation of narrative planes and through a constant
juxtaposition of the real and the imaginary, the natural and the nonnatural.
For example, the complaints of the workers about terrible working conditions,
lack of sanitary facilities, medical services, and so forth, which ended in the
workers' general strike, were the issues in the Ciénega region in Colombia in
1928. These issues are described in hyperbolic terms and intermingle with the
general plot of the family story and the reader is forced to reconstruct both
historical issues and narrative story. In the strike, characters of Macondo
interact with characters of other Latin American novels. Thus, among the

---

[10]Lucila Inés Mena, "La huelga de la compañía bananera," offers a
detailed account of the historical facts. Concerning the actions of the United
Fruit Company Jorge Eliécer Gaitán posed this complaint to the Colombian
Congress: "Las aguas también están controladas por la empresa... Así, la
compañía usa ilegalmente las aguas del río Fundación, y se construyó un dique
hasta Santa Ana con el fin de inundar todas las fincas bananeras de los
colombianos" (qtd. in Villaveces 56).

union leaders are José Arcadio Segundo and Lorenzo Gavilán, a character from Carlos Fuentes's *La muerte de Artemio Cruz*, which deals with the Mexican revolution. What is more, social problems of Macondo are juxtaposed to Meme's tragic love affair which seems initially unimportant:

> Los acontecimientos que habían de darle el golpe mortal a Macondo empezaban a vislumbrarse cuando llevaron a la casa al hijo de Meme Buendía. La situación pública era entonces tan incierta, que nadie tenía el espíritu dispuesto para ocuparse de escándalos privados. (249)

When the workers' uprisings start, her son Aureliano Babilonia is a year old. Although read as a distracting episode, the child's presence will be consequential for the denouement of the story since he will decipher the historical reality and meaning of events at the end of the novel. Through the story of the Buendías, the story of Latin American society is revised—its myths and prejudices, its dreams and failures.

José Arcadio Segundo was among the crowd that was awaiting the arrival of the civil and military leader of the province to solve the banana workers' problem and thus was a witness when the captain of the army gave the order to fire, after having read "el Decreto Número 4" signed by general Carlos Cortes Vargas (258). In the exposition made by Gaitán the details given of the massacre correspond to what we read in García Márquez's novel (Villaveces, 55). Mena shows that the words of the "Decreto Número 4" presented in *Cien años* are those read in the city of Ciénega, Colombia, after the massacre of the workers in December, 1928 ("La huelga de la compañía" 390).

After the massacre, José Arcadio Segundo wakes up in "un tren interminable y silencioso" full of corpses piled up "en el orden y el sentido en que se transportaban los racimos de banano" (260), and he realizes that the corpses of men, women, and children will be thrown into the sea like "el banano de rechazo" (261). Here there is a double discourse which permits us to see the social underpinning of the marvelous surface. The comparison of the corpses with bananas is an implicit criticism of the exploitation not only of the land and the fruit, but also of people, who were considered one more commodity to the banana company. As Fernando Ainsa states, that train:

> se lleva al final los cadáveres del personaje "colectivo" de Macondo masacrado por el poder "central" lejano.
> Los mensajeros que han cruzado las ciénagas son finalmente los asesinos de la inocencia, los mercaderes de la Edad de Hierro, quienes imponen los parámetros de otra identidad, teóricamente más moderna, pero en todo caso más cruel. (446)

The juxtaposition of José Arcadio Segundo's reality and the official story starts as soon as he gets off the phantasmagoric train and returns to Macondo. He tries to tell the people the number of dead he saw on the train, but, fearing governmental reprisals, they have "forgotten" the fact. This oblivion is caused by the politics of terror which make people assimilate "the official story": "Aquí no ha habido muertos" (261).

Not even his brother Aureliano Segundo believes his version of the three thousand dead. The Buendías have also assimilated the official version; from this perspective, memory and time fill a social and historical function in *Cien años de soledad*. Regarding the number of dead García Márquez states:

> I went to check how many dead there were in the banana workers' strike of 1928. It was a tremendous national scandal. It's not exactly known, but I was told about 17. For my book, 17 dead would have been a joke. I needed enough bodies to fill a train. I wanted the train instead of being loaded with bananas to be loaded with corpses. History was against me, with 17 dead. That would not even fill a wagon. So I put 3,000. (qtd. in Simons 18)

But the hyperbolic figure used by García Márquez helps to elucidate the arbitrary figures given by the official history, where numbers varied greatly. In some texts the massacre is treated as a slight casualty:

> Decretóse entonces turbado el orden público en la zona (5 de diciembre) y fue nombrado el general Cortés, jefe civil y militar de ella. En Ciénega, centro principal de la sedición, las cosas llegaron al extremo de tener que ordenarse, hecha la prevención del caso, una descarga sobre los huelguistas, entre los cuales resultaron muertos y heridos. (Ramón, *Historia de Colombia* 371)

This text is designed for high school programs in Colombia. One of the indications, at the beginning, is that those paragraphs which appear in small characters can be given just a brief reading or can be eliminated at the teacher's discretion. The strike's description is in small characters.

Hayden White tells us that "the historian must 'interpret' his data by excluding certain facts from his account as irrelevant to his narrative purpose" (52). In official histories of countries under an oppressive regime, relevant facts are changed to satisfy Governmental purposes. Fiction treating these facts plays an important role in questioning historical facts.

After the workers strike, the signing of the agreement between the military authorities and the workers is announced by Mr. Brown for a date in the future "when the rain stops." In Macondo it has not rained for three months, but when Mr. Brown announces his decision, a final plague, a terrible flood, will devastate Macondo lasting for "cuatro años, once meses y dos días" (267). One more plague on Macondo, this time sent by Mr. Brown, and after this will come its final destruction.

While rain keeps pouring on Macondo, historical details are interwoven with the domestic happenings. Thus a whole account of the extermination of the union leaders is recounted, and José Arcadio Segundo escapes. Due to the marvelous protection of Melquíades's room, he becomes invisible in the presence of the officer who searches for him, while Santa Sofía de la Piedad and Aureliano Segundo see him clearly. After that he starts deciphering Melquíades's manuscripts, and he also learns about the exact number of deaths at the workers' strike: "Son todos los que estaban en la estación...Tres mil cuatrocientos ocho" (285). Later he will teach all that he knows to Aureliano Babilonia, Meme's illegitimate child. On the one hand, if fear of reprisals originates oblivion; on the other, José Arcadio Segundo revindicates history by preserving memory. Thus there is the opposition of the written text and oral tradition. Towards the end of the novel, the individual convinced of the truth will become more effective than those succumbing to official oblivion. There is an explicit discourse condemning the actions of the government; José Arcadio Segundo:

> Enseñó al pequeño Aureliano a leer y a escribir, lo inició en el estudio de los pergaminos, y le inculcó una interpretación tan personal de lo que significó para Macondo la compañía bananera, que muchos años después cuando Aureliano se incorporara al mundo, había de pensarse que contaba una versión alucinada, porque era radicalmente contraria a la falsa que los historiadores habían admitido, y consagrado en los textos escolares. (296)

With Aureliano Babilonia both realities will survive: the story of the family and the "other" history, that of the exploitation, repression and massacre of the workers which will transcend the limits of Macondo. In fact, on one of his trips to the Catalonian's bookstore, while passing by one of the houses of the old banana company, he answers a telephone that is ringing:

> El lo descolgó, entendió lo que una mujer angustiada y remota preguntaba en inglés, y le contestó que sí, que la huelga había terminado, que los tres mil muertos habían sido echados al mar, que la compañía bananera se había ido, y que Macondo estaba por fin en paz desde hacía muchos años. (324)

This way of exposing historical facts is effective, although interwoven with family episodes and with hyperbolic and marvelous elements, the historical truth evolves in its entirety. In reading about the banana company, one discovers more than the massacre of the workers in Colombia. There have been several in Latin America—one in Ecuador in 1922 and one in El Salvador in 1931, to mention only two. The story of the United Fruit Company in Colombia reminds us of the economic dependence of many other Latin American countries suffering from the problem of neocolonialism.

Towards the end of the novel Aureliano Babilonia will confront the representative of the church with the true version of historical facts. When tormented by the certainty that he is his wife's brother, he goes to the parish house to search for his origins in the baptismal certificates. Angrily he questions the priest watching him:

> —¡Ah! —dijo—, entonces usted tampoco cree.
> —¿En qué?
> —Que el coronel Aureliano Buendía hizo treinta y dos guerras civiles y las perdió todas —contestó Aureliano—. Que el ejército acorraló y ametralló a tres mil trabajadores, y que se llevaron los cadáveres para echarlos al mar en un tren de doscientos vagones. (344)

When this scene takes place, Macondo has returned to its primal stage of the beginning because the flood washed away all vestiges of civilization; even Amaranta Ursula returning from Belgium with the goal of changing Macondo, forgets her European refinement and surrenders herself to Aureliano's love. After Amaranta Ursula's death, in the midst of an apocalyptic hurricane, Aureliano deciphers the last part of the manuscripts and understands his destiny. The last of the Buendías stands alone in a destroyed universe, and the reader is confronted with the universal duality of creation and destruction.

The novels studied in this chapter, *El reino de este mundo* and *Cien años de soledad*, are considered to date, respectively, the first and major examples of *realismo maravilloso*. This mode has become a new way of writing which, as we have seen in García Márquez's novel, allows the treatment of a whole range of complex realities.

While Alejo Carpentier's novel addresses in particular the historical problem in Haiti from the time of the French colonists to the Republican mulattoes by emphasizing the myth, religion, and cultural syncretisms in Haiti, García Márquez's imaginary Macondo possesses a plurality of problems. Carpentier opposes European values to Haitian culture. García Márquez's oppositions are multiple and complex. In the three moments we have isolated for our analysis we could consider the following dualities: science/prescience mentality, spirit/matter or faith/non-faith, official story/real facts. In *El reino de este mundo* the isotopies natural/supernatural work, particularly in Mackandal's transformations. In *Cien años de soledad* that juxtaposition is a constant; in fact the fable presents all kinds of supernatural events.

Alejo Carpentier claimed the baroque as legitimate for the art and even for the style of the Latin American writer:

> Nuestro arte siempre fue barroco... No temamos, pues, el barroquismo en el estilo, en la visión de los contextos, en la visión de la figura humana... El legítimo estilo del novelista latinoamericano actual es el barroco". (*Tientos y diferencias* 40-41)

Carpentier is well known for his baroque style, and one can observe that baroque descriptiveness has become characteristic of the writers of *realismo maravilloso* as a way of problematizing the act of narration. The techniques are varied, like the proliferation of signifiers to describe "the undescribable" (Chiampi 102). This baroque narrative strategy can be observed in García Márquez's novel construction of "mise-en-abyme." At the end of the novel the reader realizes that he is reading the text Melquíades has written, which is being deciphered by Aureliano Babilonia, and that the barriers between fiction and reality have been questioned at every step. In the fourth chapter we shall see how baroque descriptiveness is treated at all levels—in enunciation, representation, and language—in Aguilera Malta's novel *Siete lunas y siete serpientes*. In sum, the range of issues that can be encompassed within the realistic marvelous Latin American cultural referent allows the writers to express in their novels not only the games of imagination but also their cultural identity.

In this chapter we have considered two of the very well known writers of this genre. Many other Latin American writers have attempted to represent in their fictions the "total" Latin American reality. The rich blooming of the novel of the 1960s is part of the movement already started by previous writers in the early 1930s. Among them stands out the Ecuadorian José de la Cuadra whose novel *Los Sangurimas* will be analyzed in the next chapter.

A SEMINAL TEXT OF *REALISMO MARAVILLOSO* IN THE EARLY 1930s

> Form and content in discourse are one, once we
> understand that verbal discourse is a social pheno-
> menon—social throughout its entire range and in
> each and every of its factors, from the sound image
> to the furthest reaches of abstract meaning. (M. M.
> Bakhtin, *The Dialogic Imagination*)

General Background

Since the means of literature is language and language is a social
phenomenon, sociohistorical conditions can never be disregarded; this
becomes particularly relevant in the case of Ecuadorian literature of the
1930s.[1] A general background of this literature will help the reader to
properly place José de la Cuadra within Ecuadorian literary history and to
consider the significance of his work.

The liberal revolution of 1895, whose leader was General Eloy Alfaro,
marks important changes in the country and with it the emergence of a
significant group of middle class intellectuals who were open to new ideas and
conscious of social problems (among them, Manuel J. Calle, Luis A. Martínez,
Eduardo Mera and José Rafael Bustamante). The Russian and the Mexican
revolutions played an important role in the attitude of the intellectuals;
widespread political unrest, growing workers' movements, students' movements, heightened interest rates (especially in Andean countries) coupled with

---

[1]For the historical, political and socio-economic process in Ecuador during
the 1930s see Agustín Cueva's *El proceso de dominación política en el Ecuador*
(1974) and his articles: "Ecuador: 1925-1975" (1986) and "Literatura y sociedad
en el Ecuador: 1920-1960" (1988). See also Alejandro Moreano's "Capitalismo
y lucha de clases en la primera mitad del siglo XX" in *Ecuador pasado y
presente* (1982).

the Great Depression of the thirties created a crisis for intellectuals as well as for the general public. As historian Tulio Halperín Donghi explains:

> La crisis de 1929, no sólo creó a la economía latinoamericana problemas de dimensiones incomparablemente mayores que las que la precedieron; ofreció, además, en las metrópolis el espectáculo de un derrumbe económico acompañado de catástrofe social y crisis política en el que durante una docena de años pareció adivinarse el fin de un mundo. (Halperín 356)

Ecuador was no exception in this crisis, and, as Peruvian critic Luis Alberto Sánchez states, Ecuadorian writers of the 1930s, deeply concerned, were among the first to forge a new literature which reflected an American construction of historical recreation, social protest and inclusion of indigenous heritage:

> La literatura ecuatoriana vive su hora de descubrimiento. Está calando en lo ignorado, en lo inédito...y es la primera que se desembaraza del ropaje colonial. Mientras la novela chilena vive todavía en epitalamio con la naturaleza; mientras en la peruana dialogan el tono viejo del espectador con el polémico del militante aprista, que respalda sus dichos con sus hechos; mientras la mexicana atraviesa por la etapa más serena del que hizo y cuenta sus hazañas en tono de conversación de sobremesa...en el Ecuador se conjuga el ímpetu de hacer con la desorientación de no saber qué hacer... La crisis del cacao ha echado una sombra de miseria sobre Guayaquil. Como siempre, el monocultivo antecede a la angustia económica. En un medio como ése, tenía que florecer una literatura de protesta, y es la literatura de Guayaquil: literatura de protesta...vigorosa y descarnada, con un soplo doloroso y realista formidable. (qtd. in Rojas 188)

It is important to remember that events of the first decades of the century—revolutions, workers' organizations, increasing neocolonialism, anti-yankee sentiment—are highlighted in more recent fiction. Such is the fictionalized history told in *Cien años de soledad* studied in the second chapter, which refers to the years of the United Fruit Company in Colombia; the same problem in Central America is treated by Miguel Angel Asturias in his trilogy *Viento Fuerte* (1950), *El Papa verde* (1954), *Los ojos de los enterrados* (1960). Several novels focus on dictatorships: Aguilera Malta's *El*

secuestro del general (1973), Roa Bastos's *Yo el supremo* (1974), A. Carpentier's *El recurso del método* (1974), García Márquez's *El otoño del patriarca*
(1975) to mention a few.

Considering the socio-historical circumstances in Ecuador, Rojas, in his
study *La novela ecuatoriana*, identifies three periods: 1) 1830-1895, characterized by "conservadurismo" (conservatism) in politics and romanticism in
literature; 2) 1895-1925, liberal movement in politics as well as in literature;
3) after 1925, a return to socialism. The period 1895-1925 brings significant
liberal reforms with three important dates to be considered: November 1922,
September 1923, and July 1925. The first two correspond to popular
movements of protest because of the economic situation; in 1922 there was a
workers' strike in Guayaquil, and in 1923, a peasants strike in the Leito farm,
in the highlands. Both ended in terrible massacres of the workers. The
political problems continued, and in July 1925, a group of young soldiers, the
"Liga de militares jóvenes," took power after an effective and peaceful military
coup where there were neither protests nor killings (Reyes 2:777). This
revolution resulted in civic social reforms with positive changes in the
economic, administrative, and educational sectors. However, the political
situation continued to be extremely erratic, and from 1920 to 1940 there were
seventeen different heads of state in Ecuador.

Due to its different implications it is important to examine the year 1922.
First, groups of workers in the littoral area organized several protests which
culminated in a general strike in Guayaquil on November 15, 1922, that ended
in the massacre of the workers. This is the first time that the masses actively
participated. This fact is important because the workers' actions forced the
politicians to include social reforms in their premises (Pareja Diezcanseco,
Ecuador, 338). Different writers took note in one way or another of the 1922
massacre in their novels: Joaquín Gallegos Lara's *Las cruces sobre el agua*
(1946); Alfredo Pareja Diezcanseco's *Baldomera* (1938); Pedro Jorge Vera's
Los animales puros (1946). The first works of "postmodernismo"[2] also date
from this year, represented by Carrera Andrade's *El estanque inefable* and
Gonzalo Escudero's *Parábolas olímpicas*, both published in 1922. "Postmoder-

---

[2]"Postmodernismo" in Hispanic literature refers to the important direction
taken in literature after "modernismo." "Modernismo" is the literary movement
originated in Hispanic America at the end of the nineteenth century which
renovated Hispanic literature. See on this subject Sainz de Medrano's *Historia
de la literatura hispanoamericana: desde el modernismo* (1989).

nismo" is important because it is a break with old cultural patterns which opens the way to the avant garde movement in Ecuador that will reach its prime expression in the work of Pablo Palacio (1906-47) (Cueva, "Literatura y sociedad" 632). Palacio belongs to the so-called "Generación del 30" whose most important writers were José de la Cuadra, Pablo Palacio, Demetrio Aguilera Malta, Alfredo Pareja Diezcanseco, Joaquín Gallegos Lara, Enrique Gil Gilbert, Adalberto Ortiz, and Jorge Icaza. The works of these writers were essential in the development of Ecuadorian narrative.

Pablo Palacio's collection of short stories, "Un hombre muerto a puntapiés," and his novels *Débora* (1927) and *Vida del ahorcado* (1932) puzzled his readers because of his different approach towards reality. He says about literature:

> Yo entiendo que hay dos literaturas que siguen el criterio materialístico: una de lucha, de combate, y otra que puede ser simplemente expositiva... De este punto de vista, vivimos en momentos de crisis, en momento decadentista que debe ser expuesto a secas, sin comentario. Dos actitudes, pues, existen para mí en el escritor: la del encauzador y reformador...y la del expositor simplemente, y este punto de vista es el que me corresponde: el descrédito de las realidades presentes...invitar al asco de nuestra verdad actual. (qtd. in Adoum, *La gran literatura* 96-97)

As Adoum points out, the literature of Palacio is:

> una literatura que se piensa a sí misma, y que por ser 'nueva' cincuenta años más tarde comenzó a mostrar caminos a los jóvenes narradores de hoy, hartos del 'otro' realismo... Lo extraño es que Palacio se haya considerado anti-realista, y más aún que lo haya declarado en 1927, antes de que el realismo proliferara en América Latina y antes de que apareciera en el Ecuador. (Adoum 96, 99)

Social realism is expressed in Ecuadorian literature in the two following decades. Its literary antecedents are scarce and cannot constitute a tradition.

We can consider Miguel Riofrío's *La emancipada* (1863),[3] Luis A. Martínez's
A la Costa (1904), José de la Cuadra's "El desertor" (1923),[4] Fernando
Chávez's short story "La embrujada" (1923) and his novel *Plata y bronce*
(1927), and Leopoldo Benítez's short story "La mala hora" (1927). In contrast
to this scant previous production, during the 1930s and the 1940s social
realism is predominant in all sectors of the country. *Huasipungo* (1934) by
Jorge Icaza is the internationally best known novel. It is important to take into
account that there is evolution in the production of the writers. Donoso Pareja
characterizes the decade of the thirties as evolving in a spiral shape, "evolución
en espiral," with the coexistence of several expressive forms (*Los grandes* 111-
14).

The work that definitely institutes social realism in Ecuadorian literature
is the collection of short stories *Los que se van. Cuentos del cholo y del
montuvio* (1930) by Joaquín Gallegos Lara, Enrique Gil Gilbert and Demetrio
Aguilera Malta[5]. This collection is very important for the narrative that will
follow. Due to the radical changes in writing, the decolonization of language,

---

[3]Antonio Sacoto in the introduction to his 1983 edition of Miguel Riofrío's
La emancipada, which was originally published in Quito in 1863 as a serial
story of *La Unión*, establishes this work as the first Ecuadorian novel. Thus
La emancipada appeared sixteen years before Juan León Mera's *Cumandá*
(1879) which is usually considered the first Ecuadorian novel. Due to the
strong argument that *La emancipada* poses against the traditionalist mores in
the treatment of women, we can list this work as one of the antecedents for
social realism.

[4]This publication indicates that De la Cuadra as early as 1923 was already
exploring the *montuvio*'s world in order to write a literature of protest
(Robles, "La noción de la vanguardia" 653).

[5]The authors' epigraph for their book reads:
> AL FRENTE:
> Este libro no es un haz de egoísmos.
> Tiene tres autores: no tiene tres partes.
> Es una sola cosa.
> Pretende que unida sea la obra
> como fue unido el ensueño que la
> creó. Ha nacido de la marcha fraterna
> de nuestros tres espíritus. Nada más.
> Los autores.

and the recovery of popular expressions and of the free use of sexual motives—unusual for the times—the short stories caused a great impact not only in Ecuador, but also in the rest of Latin America. The characters in the stories are the marginal inhabitants of the Ecuadorian coastal region: *el cholo*, *el montuvio*, *el negro*—local types—struggling violently among themselves and with a primitive natural setting. Jorge Enrique Adoum states that this book:

> inaugura el nuevo relato ecuatoriano, orienta su estética, determina su actitud y contiene, aun cuando fuera en germen, algunas de sus características esenciales: ambiente, lenguaje, situaciones, personajes. (*La gran literatura* 34)

The authors of *Los que se van*, faithful to their beliefs, defended their position towards art despite all the polemics that arose because of their work.[6] Soon after the publication of this book, José de la Cuadra and Alfredo Pareja Diezcanseco joined these writers in forming the "Grupo de Guayaquil."[7] The writers of this group, at a very young age—De la Cuadra had been nineteen years old, Aguilera Malta and Pareja Diezcanseco, fourteen; Gallegos Lara, eleven and Gil Gilbert, ten—were marked by the bloody episode of 1922 (Pareja Diezcanseco, "Los narradores" 692).

Working as a team, the five members of the group were productive. Although they did not publish joint works, nevertheless they shared ideological

---

[6]Angel F. Rojas states, "De inmediato se tildó a la literatura que hacían los autores del discutido libro, como el producto de un plan político, que buscaba producir el escándalo internacional, el desprestigio de nuestro medio retrasado, revelando imprudentemente detalles vergonzosos de la explotación del hombre campesino y describiendo a éste como una especie de subhombre movido por la lujuria, los celos, el alcohol y a ratos, por el instinto homicida" (185).

[7]Jorge Icaza establishes three groups of writers with a unified attitude towards that reality: "El Grupo de Guayaquil" with José de la Cuadra, Joaquín Gallegos Lara, Demetrio Aguilera Malta, Enrique Gil Gilbert, and Alfredo Pareja Diezcanseco; "El Grupo de Quito" with Fernando Chávez, Humberto Salvador, Jorge Fernández, Enrique Terán, Jorge Icaza; and "El Grupo el Austro" with G. h. Mata, Alfonso Cuesta y Cuesta, Angel F. Rojas, and Pablo Palacio ("Relato, espíritu unificador" 211-16). However, as noted by Rojas (189), only the "Grupo de Guayaquil" worked with homogeneity as a "team."

and artistic interests. José de la Cuadra, who had previously published several short stories and had more experience and a sharp critical judgement, acted as the leader of the group. Always a novelist, Alejo Pareja Diezcanseco never wrote short stories. Enrique Gil Gilbert and Demetrio Aguilera Malta published novels after the volume of short stories. Gallegos Lara, although he did not publish, wrote and worked continuously with the group; he was the more structured and demanding of the three authors of *Los que se van* (Angel F. Rojas, 193). Soon the group became very well known and attracted international attention.[8] Towards the end of the 1940s, after the death of José de la Cuadra (1941) and Joaquín Gallegos Lara (1947), the group stopped its literary activities as a team. However Aguilera Malta and Pareja Diezcanseco continued to write and to publish. Today there is no doubt that the work of this group was important.

Since the focus of this study is on the discourse of *realismo maravilloso* I shall consider in this chapter an early example of this discourse in José de la Cuadra's *Los Sangurimas*.

José de la Cuadra's *Los Sangurimas*

> Si no hubiéramos leyendas, acaso habría que inventarlas. Metafóricamente, un pueblo sin pasado mítico, es como un hombre que jamás ha sido niño. (José de la Cuadra)

As was seen in the previous chapter, Alejo Carpentier and Gabriel García Márquez are recognized as canonical writers of the discourse of *realismo maravilloso*. The antecedents of this discourse, however, can be traced to José de la Cuadra's *Los Sangurimas*, published in 1934. In this novel, written in the decade when socio-realistic literature predominated in Ecuador, De la Cuadra does not attempt to represent reality in a mirror-like fashion, as did many of his social-realist contemporaries; rather, he "interprets" reality artistically, incorporating marvelous elements into a text, while still managing to refer to and comment upon actual social problems. Thus his novel presents mythical,

---

[8]Shortly after the group of five was formed, Angel F. Rojas, Adalberto Ortiz and Pedro Jorge Vera joined the group. In this study only the writers of the initial group are considered.

hyperbolic and magico-realistic elements which are characteristic of the contemporary Latin American narrative.

De la Cuadra, an indefatigable reader, who was familiar with the European and American literary movements of the time, experiments in *Los Sangurimas* with the amalgamation of marvelous and real elements in order to convey the entirety of the *montuvio*'s world he knew well. Three years after the publication of this novel De la Cuadra published the essay *El montuvio ecuatoriano* (1937),[9] where he explains and systematizes the principles that govern the world presented in *Los Sangurimas*. This essay is an excellent sociological study of the *montuvio*, inhabitant of the Ecuadorian lowland tropic. In it De la Cuadra describes the *montuvio* zone as a huge and fertile hinterland where there is a predominance of "latifundios" (large landed estates). The racial hybridism of the *montuvios* includes 60% Indian, 30% Negro and 10% white. De la Cuadra explains how, isolated in their region, the *montuvios* are attached to their land and their mythical customs. They form a closed nucleus where sentimental life revolves around the mother and social prestige around the father whose word is the law. The *montuvios* have a particular sense for justice, politics, sex and life in general. They do not have certain social taboos; for example, for them, incest is not a taboo (*Obras completas* 863-908).

In *Los Sangurimas*, *La Hondura* is the microcosm of the *montuvio*'s world, whose world view is radically different from our own. In this world myth and reality are inseparable; they form one unity as is the case in the primitive cultures of Central America and the Caribbean, which are exemplified in literary works such as *Hombres de maíz* (1949), *El reino de este mundo* (1948), and *Cien años de soledad* (1967).

The introduction to *Los Sangurimas* is "a theory," "Teoría del Matapalo," which allows the reader to anticipate what will be developed in the novel. De la Cuadra's method is innovative, for he uses the image of the "Matapalo"—a magnificent tree of the Ecuatorial tropic which devours whatever is near its domains—to portray in his novel the unrestricted power exercised by Nicasio Sangurima and his family. With this family the author exemplifies the *montuvio*'s reality—a mixture of legends, anecdotes, violence and mystery.

In the novel, the tree has a "strange, spectral and mysterious life" similar to that of the *montuvios*. The tragedy of Los Sangurimas, which will be developed only in the last part of the novel, is already announced in this theory in the form of a storm which shakes this strong tree:

---

[9]References to this text as well as to the other works by De la Cuadra correspond to *Obras completas* (1958).

> El matapalo es árbol montuvio. Recio, formidable, se hunde
> profundamente en el agro con sus raíces semejantes a garras... El
> pueblo montuvio es así como el matapalo, que es una reunión de
> árboles, un consorcio de árboles, tantos como troncos.
>
> La gente Sangurima de esta historia es una familia montuvia en
> el pueblo montuvio: un árbol de tronco añoso, de fuertes ramas y
> hojas campeantes a las cuales cierta vez sacudió la tempestad. (451)

Two elements can be considered of structural value in the novel: the tree
and incest. Nicasio Sangurima, the "tronco añoso," is the axis of the novel.
Genealogy is important, and the reader learns about the life of five generations of Sangurimas as well as the creation and destruction of a mythical
place: *La Hondura* whose name denotes serious problems.[10] Incest can be
traced throughout the novel not as a curse on the family, as is the case in *Cien
años de soledad*, but as an integral part of the *montuvio*'s reality.

De la Cuadra organizes *Los Sangurimas* into three parts, each named
after the parts of the tree: trunk, branches, and leaves. Time and space are
fragmented, there are multiple narrative planes, and there is no sequence
from one chapter to the next in the first two parts. During the narration there
are different prolepses and analepses which call the reader's attention to the
text.[11] Prolepses and analepses are important because they shed light on
antecedents, or they are brief allusions to events that will be told in the future,
or they complete the information on facts already stated. Part Three, where
the Sangurimas' tragedy takes place, has a linear sequence. Violence and
power recur as leitmotif in each part of the novel.

The violent story of Nicasio's origin—crime and exodus—is told in Part
One, "El tronco añoso" (the aged trunk). Nicasio Sangurima is the son of a
montuvia and a foreigner who raped her while her brothers were absent. On
their return, one of the brothers defended the "honor" of the family and killed
the foreigner. Nicasio's mother, in turn, killed this brother. Violence among
the siblings stopped because of fear of their father. Afraid of her relatives'
vengeance the woman escaped with little Nicasio to a remote place where she

---

[10]"Hondura" means depth, profundity but it also has a figurative meaning.
"Meterse en honduras" is to get into trouble. To deal with difficult things
without enough knowledge of them (*Diccionario ideológico a la lengua
española*; 2a ed.).

[11]To avoid the psychological connotation of the terms "anticipation" and
"retrospection," Gérard Genette adopts the terms "prolepses" and "analepses."
These are the terms we will use in our analysis. See his *Narrative Discourse.
An Essay in Method* 33-85.

founded *La Hondura* (451-476). Thus the importance of patriarchal authority and the generalized practice of violence are established from the beginning.

In Part Two, "Las ramas robustas" (the strong branches) the reader learns about four of Nicasio's children: Ventura, Terencio, Francisco, and Eufrasio. All are extraordinary. Everything is possible in *La Hondura*—incest, murders, endless parties and drunkenness, fighting over women, and so on (477-496). No exterior interference disturbs life in this place; however, once outside forces enter, this world collapses.

This is shown in Part Three, "Torbellino en las hojas" (whirlwind in the leaves), when three of Ventura's children—María Mercedes, María Victoria and María Julia—who are studying in Guayaquil, come back to *La Hondura* for a vacation. María Victoria is killed by her cousins, "Los Rugeles," Eufrasio's children. The Rural Police intervene and apprehend the criminals, and Nicasio's invincible power comes to an end. This is the tragedy announced in the theory as a storm (497-513). *La Hondura*, like *Comala*, *Macondo*, or *Santorontón*, is a marvelous and mysterious world in which extraordinary creatures dwell.[12]

Lexically, marvelous has two different meanings, according to *Webster's Ninth New Collegiate Dictionary*: 1) "unusual, extraordinary;" 2) "supernatural, magic." The first meaning implies a quantitative difference from humans. It includes any exaggeration or unusual conditions compared to human norms. In the second meaning, the nature of marvelous has a qualitative difference from humans, for it is produced by the intervention of supernatural forces and does not have a rational explanation.[13] These lexical definitions of the marvelous help us to understand its manifestations in Hispanic American narrative. In some novels, circumstances and characters are simply extraordinary (*Los pasos perdidos*); in others, the marvelous appears as supernatural (*Pedro Páramo*), and finally there are novels where there is an amalgamation of both the supernatural and the extraordinary (Chiampi, 48). We saw this in *Cien años de soledad* analyzed in the second chapter of this study. In *Los*

---

[12]Already in 1931 De la Cuadra had created a mythical space in his unfinished novel *Los monos enloquecidos* which tells the extraordinary incidents of Gustavo Hernádez's life. Editorial Casa de la Cultura Ecuatoriana published the novel in 1951. See Adoum's comment in *Obras completas* 618. For a discussion of this novel see Robles's *Testimonio* 153-70.

[13]For Todorov the marvelous unfolds into the fantastic-marvelous, "the class of narratives that are presented as fantastic and that end with an acceptance of the supernatural" and the "marvelous in the pure state which has no distinct frontiers" (*The Fantastic* 52, 53).

Sangurimas, we find an early attempt to amalgamate the supernatural and the extraordinary. Nicasio, who—according to people's comments—presents extraordinary and supernatural characteristics (following the second meaning of the marvelous), becomes a mythical figure. The other characters as well as the horrible circumstances of the crime described in the third part are unusual and extraordinary (following the first meaning of the marvelous).

"El tronco añoso" (the old trunk). There are seven chapters in this part, each formed by short episodes. Facts are recounted by old Nicasio, by a third person narrator, or by members of the audience who have either witnessed the marvelous facts or who have heard about them. Thus collective memory is constituted. This collective memory becomes important in the process of the mythification of Nicasio. Narrator, narratee, and cultural context are significant. De la Cuadra's new structure and his use of different voices[14] are an anticipation of the attempt to capture total reality by different strategies in representation, so common in contemporary Latin American narrative.[15]

The juxtaposition of marvelous and real elements is important for the construction of Nicasio's character. Since what the community believes

----

[14]The concept of "voice" developed by Gérard Genette in his *Narrative Discourse* 212-62 has also been useful for our study.

[15]Several critics point out the relation of *Los Sangurimas* to elements in contemporary narrative. The best treatment to our knowledge is René de Costa's "Reflexiones sobre el personaje de configuración mítica 'vis a vis' la novela Hispanoamericana dicha nueva." Jacques Gilard's "De *Los Sangurimas* a *Cien años de soledad*" presents points central to both novels like incest, the crime and exodus, the repetition of names and characters; however, his insistence at the beginning and at the end of his article that he believes García Márquez never read De la Cuadra's work, diminishes the force of his statements. What is important is to establish the uniqueness of De la Cuadra's novel which was written in 1934. Fernando Alegría in an interview with Demetrio Aguilera Malta ("Diálogo con Fernando Alegría") and later in his *Nueva historia de la novela hispanoamericana* (298), recommends that the admirers of the Buendías give "una buena mirada a *Los Sangurimas*"; however, he does not develop any details. Humberto E. Robles in his book on De la Cuadra comments: "La presencia de lo maravilloso, de la hipérbole y del humor que se revela en este texto [*Los Sangurimas*] permiten pensar en cuánto anticipa Cuadra los métodos del colombiano" (213). Antonio Sacoto in *La nueva novela ecuatoriana* (22-23) also comments on the topic and quotes De Costa.

constitutes the marvelous and because all the deeds occurred in a remote time in the past, Nicasio becomes a mythical figure. The use of the imperfect tense by an anonymous narrator creates a distance and is effective for this purpose. "De ño Nicasio se referían cosas extravagantes y truculentas" (456)—announces the narrator, as an introduction to the extraordinary characteristics people attribute to Nicasio. The narrative voice shifts to different characters in the audience who corroborate the marvelous facts. To build up the legend around this character De la Cuadra uses themes from popular folklore like the "oración del Justo Juez"[16] or the "entierros."[17] He also uses the well known theme of the pact with the devil. The incorporation of the *montuvio*'s voice: its popular expressions, its own syntactic and linguistic conventions is one of De la Cuadra's artistic accomplishments. This is what an eye witness relates about Nicasio's power to kill distant enemies:

> La montonera de Venancio Ramos tenía preso en un brusquero lejísimo a Jaén... El viejo Sangurima supo y rezó la oración del Justo Juez. "Ya verán cómo se les afloja Jaén", dijo. Después sacó el revólver y disparó al aire. Se rió. "Esta bala le ha llegado al corazón al pelado Ramos"... Al otro día llegó a Quevedo el capitán Jaén... "¿Cómo te zafaste Jaén?" "Ahí verán, pues; ni yo mismo sé." "¿Y qué es del pelado Venancio?" "Gusanera. Una bala que salió del monte lo mató". Ño Sangurima preguntó: "Donde le pegó la bala?" "En la noble; me creo que el corazón habrá sido". Ño Sangurima se golpeó

---

[16]This prayer according to popular belief has magic powers and has been used by Spanish writers since the XVI century. Américo Castro in his notes to Quevedo's *El Buscón* I (74) alludes to the popularity of this prayer in Spain and Portugal during the XVI and XVII centuries. This prayer was adopted by the black witches in Latin America, and it is still popular today particularly in the criminal world. See Fernando Ortiz, *Hampa afro-cubana. Los negros brujos* (89-91). Alejo Carpentier also uses it in *El reino de este mundo*. Solimán, among other magic prayers for Leclerc's health, recommends to Paulina "la del Gran Juez" (76). De la Cuadra takes advantage of the marvelous element of this prayer. José Eustasio Rivera and Ciro Alegría mentioned this prayer in their novels before De la Cuadra, but they do not develop its possibilities (Robles, *Testimonio* 212).

[17]This refers to the place where people have buried their money or jewelry. It is believed that there are many places in Ecuador where there are buried treasures. People who dare to profane the "entierros" die by the hands of the "huaco"—the phantom keeper of these treasures (Barriga López, *Los mitos en la región andina* 115).

la barriga de gusto. "Todavía tengo buena puntería, carajo", dijo. (459-60)

By contrast with the fantastic where the main characteristic is the doubt of the reader about the events described (Todorov, 83) in *realismo maravilloso* there is no hesitation. To achieve this, real and marvelous events are described on the same level, without antinomy. In the above paragraph the logically impossible action of Nicasio killing with a bullet someone who is in a different town is presented as the logical consequence of his prayer "la oración del Justo Juez." The marvelous is an integral part of the *montuvio*'s world, thus Nicasio's actions are accepted by the community without questioning. Expressions like "claro," "así ha de ser," "ahá," indicate their natural acknowledgment of the marvelous reality. The reader does not question the facts either because they apply to a culture where the imaginary coexists with the real. The richness of Nicasio's land also belongs to the marvelous. He made a pact with the devil; later he deceived the devil by hiding the document of the pact in the cemetery which is a sacred place. The devil retaliates and does not allow Nicasio to die. Thus this explains his longevity (460-61). Another marvelous characteristic is Nicasio's ability to talk with dead people. He usually talks with his two former wives who died many years before (466) and another dead person, Rigoberto Zambrano, revealed to him the place of his "entierro." Thus one understands the source of his great fortune (462-63).

In all the above instances, the narrative accounts for the *montuvio*'s point of view where the marvelous prevails. A comparison of the text with what De la Cuadra stated three years later in *El montuvio ecuatoriano* gives us the idea of his artistic elaboration of that reality. The legendary stories about Nicasio Sangurima are told on different occasions by presumed "witnesses" whose imaginations keep adding unusual traits to his figure until he becomes an extraordinary character both feared and admired. Gathered at night, drinking coffee (456), people talk about him in the same way De la Cuadra—depicting the mythical characteristics of the *montuvios*—describes it happens in real life:

En las bellas noches tropicales, reunidos en la cocina alrededor del fogón donde hierve el agua para el café puro, los montuvios cuentan las "penaciones" y los "ejemplos". Poe no habría desdeñado aprovechar los argumentos de las unas; y, Vorágine habría aplicado los otros a algunos de los santos de su Leyenda Dorada. (*Obras completas* 884-85)

Juxtaposed with the marvelous actions people attribute to Nicasio come the 'true' facts of the story narrated by him in humorous and hyperbolic terms. This account is also extraordinary and thus reinforces the *montuvio*'s point of view.

In this patriarchal community "machismo" is of capital importance and is proved by the number of children, by courageous acts and by violence. Thus, Nicasio exaggerates his "qualities" and assures that his innumerable children—by different women—are scattered all over the country (464). Thus his extraordinary virility is also a measure of his power. As proof of his courage he keeps his coffin under his bed along with the bones of his former two wives with whom—he affirms—he sleeps and talks periodically. When people ask him if he is not afraid of his dead wives he answers with humor:

> —Uno le tendrá miedo a lo que no conoce, pero a lo que se conoce no. ¡Qué miedo les voy a tener a mis mujeres! No dirá usté que no las conozco hasta donde más adentro se puede. (466)

Nicasio represents the *montuvio* who lives in a world of his own with no outside interference. As the master of *La Hondura*, he acts arbitrarily and does not follow the law. Every time he has a problem he imposes his will by violence or by bribery—his best lawyer is "el billete" (474-76). With the figure of Nicasio, De la Cuadra criticizes not only the violent and arbitrary exercise of power but also a corrupted system that has prevailed for decades. Nicasio knows that his word is the law; nobody can contradict him, for this has been the tradition of the family. Recalling his grandfather, he says: "Porque lo que el papás de mi mama mandaba, era la ley de Dios" (456). He takes pride in his own attitude after his mother's death:

> —Cuando mi mama me dejó pa irse al cielo, yo era mocetón no más. Pero, claro, era un Sangurima enterito, sin que me faltara un pelo... Enseguida empecé a mandar... Dije: "Lo que se es en esta posesión, naidien me ningunea". Y naidien me ningunió... (474)

Exercise of power means to impose his own order, thus Nicasio does not trust any authority and because his word is the law, he does not have a written will. He gives his orders orally to his oldest son Ventura:

> —Papeles ¿pa qué? Si estuviera vivo mi hijo abogao, bueno. Pero, de no... Este hijo doctor había muerto tiempo atrás en circunstancias horribles. (470)

The prolepsis of the death of his son, the lawyer, is one of the devices that, as was explained before, contributes to the unity of the diegesis. In Part Two, the lawyer's death will be depicted in all of its horrible details, and, in Part Three, María Victoria will be murdered in the same geographical space. The circumstances of the crime will also be horrible.

De la Cuadra depicts Nicasio with his good and bad traits as he envisaged that the *montuvio* should be understood: "Y hay que abarcarlo tal y como es, en todas sus dimensiones, con sus virtudes y sus defectos, con sus grandezas y sus mezquindades" (*Obras completas* 908).

One of Nicasio's positive traits is the sense of justice regarding the distribution of the land among all of his children. He has already divided it, in equal parts, among his legitimate and illegitimate children. However, as Nicasio is the absolute ruler it is understood that his children will take possession of the land only after his death (470). Another positive characteristic of this character is his ability to love unconditionally. His love is expressed as reverence for the memory of his mother (662), as favoritism for his son Eufrasio (490), and as blind justification for the actions of Los Rugeles (508). As will be seen in Part Three, this blind love for his grandchildren will eventually cause his final destruction.

After the presentation of Nicasio comes that of his domain, *La Hondura*, the closed world where the action takes place. The geographical space is also described by juxtaposing real and marvelous isotopies. This parallelism highlights the figure of the patriarch, he and his domain are unique. Nobody knows the limits of *La Hondura*: "Ni su propietario conocía su verdadera extensión" (466). Because the law responds to Nicasio's will and need for expansion, the endless extension of the land mirrors his unlimited power.

Not only the extension of the land but also its richness mirrors his owner's power. The property is crossed by the river "Mameyes" which has marvelous qualities that make the soil extraordinarily fertile (467). Nicasio makes humorous remarks, restating the fantastic richness of the soil: "En *La Hondura* hay partes pa sembrarlo todo. **Hace uno un hueco, mete una piedra, y sale un árbol de piedras**" (469; emphasis added).

The river's current which in this first part gives life and richness to the soil will be the last resource the patriarch plans to use to rescue his grandchildren in the third part. As will be seen, his plan fails, and Nicasio's power comes to an end.

The house, as the residence of power, functions as the center of this universe and responds to Nicasio's need for expansion and assertion of authority. It has been remodeled several times. It has an excellent location with regard to landscape, light and water. It is described in hyperbolic terms:

> La casa grande de la hacienda estaba magníficamente situada a la orilla del río... **La casa era enorme, anchurosa, con cuartos inmensos, con galerías extensísimas.**
>
> Las fachadas estaban **acribilladas** de ventanas. Entraban al interior el aire y el sol **con una desmesurada abundancia.** (471, emphasis added)

Reinforcing the centrality of power and also social stratification Nicasio's house is surrounded only by the houses of his legitimate children. Thus the house and its surroundings are the "sacred zone" reserved for the privileged. The illegitimate children live far from *La Hondura* (470). This circular privileged space where power resides brings to our mind the famous chalk circle where only Colonel Aureliano Buendía could enter in *Cien años de soledad*.

A constant among Nicasio's preoccupations is his continuous search for origins, for cultural identity. Within the house there is also a sacred place, "el mirador" (the watchtower), which is reserved for Nicasio. There he sits at dusk to contemplate his domain and to evoke his past and reconsider his life. It is no accident that the bell of the watchtower is called "Perpetua" (everlasting). The remembrance of his mother which never abandons him is here stronger than ever (471). His mother was an extraordinary woman. There is a drastic contrast between her and the rest of the women presented in the novel. This difference will be discussed in the third part of this chapter.

After the description of *La Hondura* and its organization this first part ends with an analepsis. In the last episode, "Líos judiciales," Nicasio tells his grandchildren how, after his mother's death, he made changes in the property. As master of his land, by force or bribery, he imposed his own rules on the region without paying attention to the official law (474-76).

The movement of the narrative in this first part is circular. It starts with Nicasio's recollections before an audience, and it ends with his recollections before his children. De la Cuadra sets out the principles which will later bring unity to the story, and he establishes what will be a constant: the father's word is the only law, and violence gives the Sangurimas power. In accurate and economic prose he provides only the essentials, but the reader already has a clear idea of the *montuvio*'s world. Nicasio Sangurima, like the "Matapalo," is the strong trunk around which everything develops. The opposition of marvelous and natural isotopies is effective in creating the mythical figure of the patriarch in a world where violence, fantasy, exaggeration, and humor are integral parts. The narrative technique which uses recollections of the characters permits the fragmentation of time and space, and the reader is forced to construct the chronology.

"Las ramas robustas" (The Strong Branches). The same juxtaposition of marvelous/real is followed in the second part of the novel. Among the sixteen legitimate children of Nicasio Sangurima, the narrator pays attention only to four who have extraordinary characteristics: Ventura, "El acuchillado;" Terencio, "El padre cura;" Francisco, "El abogado;" and Eufrasio, "El coronel." They are the strong branches of the Sangurima family.

These four unusual characters belong to the first definition of marvelous, because they are extraordinary people due to their extravagant behavior, but they do not incorporate supernatural elements. There is exaggeration and humor in the description of these characters, and in many instances incest is suggested. In "Bejucos" (lianas), the last chapter of this second part, there is a reference to the common children—"montuvios rancios con los vicios y virtudes de las gentes litorales y **sin nada de extraordinario**" (496, emphasis added). Thus juxtaposed to the extraordinary children are the common children. In this way the description of these characters follows the same pattern of juxtaposition as in the first part.

Only one among the common children is mentioned: Felipe "chancho rengo," who lives with and has children by his sister Melania. This incest is known and admitted openly even by Nicasio who comments without judging: "-¡Y yo qué voy a hacer! Yo no mando en el fundillo de naidien" (496). Nicasio acknowledges the fact without questioning it because incest is part of their culture. Felipe represents the common *montuvio* for whom incest is not a taboo.

Each of the four brothers is described in a separate chapter, but a structural technique which lends unity to the whole allows that the description of each character include a reference to the next one to come. When describing Ventura, the narrator mentions his closeness to Terencio; this one says a mass in memory of Francisco, the lawyer, whom people believe was murdered by Eufrasio. These references make logical the transition from one character to the other.

Ventura, the oldest son, De la Cuadra portrays as a character in conflict. He shows how absolute is the patriarchal authority. Ventura manifests a blind submission to his father which is rooted in a traumatic experience from his childhood (478). There is a great contrast between his "sinister" physical aspect and his way of life which does not follow all the community's common rules. On the one hand, like the rest of the *montuvios*, Ventura believes that virility is shown in the number of children. Thus he has twenty-four children (478). However he is not promiscuous, which is one of the characteristics of "machismo"; all his children are by the same woman, his wife. Unlike the other *montuvios*, he does not show violence as the dominant rule in his life. On the other hand, he dreams of a different future for his three daughters who are studying in Guayaquil. In *La Hondura*, according to patriarchal codes, female characters are marginalized, reduced to the sphere of the house, destined only to have children. Ventura's preoccupation with having his daughters educated, does not follow the regular rule of the *montuvio*'s world, where women stay at home. As we shall see in the last part of the novel, Ventura's breaking with the *montuvio*'s patriarchal canon will result in tragic consequences.

Terencio, "El padre cura," who is the religious authority of *La Hondura*, is Ventura's closest brother and his companion of endless inebriations. The juxtaposition of religion and materialism, sacred and profane, is typical for this priest who knows neither moral nor physical restrictions. The religion he preaches is to suit the people in that area, "entre sus ideas más peregrinas estaba la de que había que democratizar el dogma" (484). Terencio is not the canonical religious figure: he likes obscenities in the jokes he tells, the books he reads, and the records he plays. In *La Hondura*—like the other Sanguri-mas—Terencio has a house. A beautiful girl and a child live in that house; they figure sometimes as his niece and nephew and other times as his godchildren (482). Here, there is also the incestuous pattern—although not in a direct line—in the presumed kinship because of his relationship with "a niece" or a "godchild." Since there is no physical description of this priest, his figure can be seen as a parodic critique of religion (Robles, *Testimonio* 229). Terencio's characterization is well along the anticlerical lines of Ecuadorian literature of protest. A critique of religion via the character of the priest can also be observed in: Luis A. Martinez's *A la costa* (1904), Jorge Icaza's *Huasipungo* (1934), Alejandro Carrión's "La manzana dañada" (1948).

Francisco, "El abogado" (the lawyer), is the son Nicasio had sent to study law in hopes that he would resolve his legal problems, but he was unable to do so. Thus he will pay the consequences, as does anyone who does not fulfill patriarchal expectations. Francisco has two outstanding characteristics: his extreme love for solitude, despite his fear of being killed, and his unusual sexual behavior:

> El doctor era una acerba especie de cenobita. Por su modo de ser se había ganado algunas leyendas acerca de su naturaleza sexual... **Gustaba de la soledad en una forma exagerada** (emphasis added). En realidad, era una manía. Pues, según se afirmaba, sufría grandes miedos en la soledad, siempre temiendo que lo asesinaran.
>
> Su muerte se le anunciaba como un presagio fatal, que hubo de cumplirse. (488)

In this chapter, Francisco's death, mentioned as a prolepsis in the first part, is described in all of its horrible details. There is, however, ambiguity regarding Francisco's death. Reflecting on comments that Don Nicasio ordered the crime and Eufrasio executed it, the narrator states:

> De examinar desapasionadamente el asunto, advertíase que ninguna causa aparente existía para acusar de la muerte del doctor Sangurima a su hermano el coronel. (486)

The mystery of Francisco's death is never resolved in the narrative. Yet with this ambiguity something is clear: Francisco—representative of external law—who could not accomplish things according to Nicasio's wishes, had to disappear from the closed world of *La Hondura*.

Nicasio Sangurima prefers those who can impose themselves on others. Thus his favorite son is Eufrasio, "El coronel," who is the military authority in *La Hondura*. He is very much like his father in terms of physical traits and preferences: power, imposition by violence, numerous children by different women and so on (490). Eufrasio has also a legend, not for his supernatural powers, but for his violent deeds. Thus, although he does not become a mythical figure as his father, his acts make him stand out and be feared. As will be seen in the third part of the novel, following the tradition of the family, imposition by violence is also the characteristic of Eufrasio's children, Los Rugeles, Nicasio's beloved grandchildren.

If with Nicasio, De la Cuadra criticizes the abuses of power by part of the owners of latifundiums—characteristic of the rural societies in Latin America—with Eufrasio Sangurima he criticizes politics, specifically "la montonera,"[18] which refers to the interventions of the *montuvio* in politics. Colonel Eufrasio Sangurima—like Colonel Aureliano Buendía three decades later in *Cien años de soledad*—has participated in all the revolutions of the country, and he does not trust governmental politics:

No había habido revolución en los últimos tiempos a la cual no hubiera asistido el coronel Eufrasio Sangurima.

En cuanto llegaba a sus oídos la noticia de que algún caudillo se había alzado en armas contra el Gobierno, el coronel Eufrasio Sangurima se sentía aludido.

—Yo estoy con los de abajo —decía—. Todo el que está mandando es enemigo del pueblo honrado. (492)

"El coronel" and his group are feared by the people of the country because they can get anything by the imposition of violence. Eufrasio's final career—as

---

[18]The origins of this term are explained in De la Cuadra's *El montuvio ecuatoriano*:

La montonera se origina en la explotación de la tendencia mítica del montuvio.

Creado el héroe militar, por lo corriente—cualquier gamonal, o individuo que aspira a serlo, decide "levantarse." Reúne bajo su mando gente voluntaria...se acoge al nombre del héroe como a una bandera, y se lanza a combatir a las fuerzas regulares en guerra de guerrillas. Si triunfa el pretendiente en todo el país y se trepa al sillón quiteño, el cabecilla de montonera ocupará una situación privilegiada...si pasa al revés, regresarán los sobrevientes acompañados de su glorioso jefe, se internarán en las selvas y se dedicarán al vandalaje. (*Obras completas* 892)

usually happens with the "montoneros"—is as a horse thief. When he stops fighting, he retires to his house and his children, all of whom—as a sign of his "machismo"—are by different women: "vivía ahora en el caserío de la hacienda, junto a una turbamulta de hijos suyos, de distintas madres, por supuesto" (494).

De la Cuadra states that *La Hondura* reproduces the village of this area where the patriarch replaces the civil authority: "una aldeúca montuvia donde el teniente político estaba reemplazado por el patriarca familiar" (497). Considering this, the patriarch's four extraordinary children also represent specific figures well known in the small Latin American villages. Ventura is the greedy owner; Terencio, the licentious priest; Francisco, the dishonest lawyer and Eufrasio the ignorant colonel whose only law is violence (Adoum, "El fetiche" 33). Thus De la Cuadra is not only exposing the life and mores of the region but he is also criticizing the abuses of an organizational system which reaches broader limits. As will be analyzed in the fourth chapter, Aguilera Malta treats the same motive, using contemporary narrative techniques, in *Siete lunas y siete serpientes*.

Ventura, Terencio, and Eufrasio are characters that play a specific role in the development of the facts in the last part of the novel. Thus their characterization as the strong branches of the Sangurima's tree has also a structural purpose. They provide antecedents to facts recounted in the third part where Ventura's and Eufrasio's children are the protagonists. The details of Francisco's horrible death and the geographical space where it takes place will have its echo in María Victoria's dreadful fate.

"Torbellino en las hojas" (Whirlwind in the Leaves). This part has five chapters that relate the tragedy that was announced at the beginning. The protagonists are six of Nicasio's "extraordinary" grandchildren: Pedro, Manuel and Facundo—sons of colonel Eufrasio Sangurima—known as Los Rugeles, and María Mercedes, María Victoria and María Julia—daughters of Ventura.

Los Rugeles, like their father, have a legend of violent deeds and everybody is afraid of them. Ventura's daughters are beautiful, sophisticated, coquettish and study in the city. Their coming back to *La Hondura* for a short vacation initiates the confrontation of this closed universe with the exterior world.

Contrary to the first and second parts where time and space are fragmented, here, facts are related in chronological order mainly by a third person narrator, and dialogue is minimal. De la Cuadra chooses six grandchildren of Nicasio to show the conflict between mores of the exterior world and those of the *montuvios*. After gaining the attention of their cousins, following the customs of the region, Los Rugeles want to live with them. The girls, who now have different cultural values, refuse: "Casarnos, bueno —dijeron—. Pero así, como los perros, no..." (502). Los Rugeles agree to marry, but Ventura objects that the girls need to finish their studies. This act prompts Los Rugeles to commit one of the most horrible crimes of the region: to rape and savagely murder María Victoria, their naive cousin, who, disobeying her father, has agreed to escape with them. This perverse incident is described with photographic detail in the episode "El hecho bárbaro" (507-508).

In this third part of the novel De la Cuadra exposes to its highest degree the problems and conflicts of this patriarchal society whose means for gaining power are violent. Nicasio is a product of that society and prefers those who follow that rule. Disregarding the horrendous crime, he acts cruelly towards his oldest son: "-¿Y quién sería que mató a la muchacha? Porque lo que es 'los Rugeles' no han sido, seguro" (508). Ventura with his nonviolent character does not fit into that system, and thus he becomes a victim. He stands impotent before those who hold the power, Nicasio and Colonel Eufrasio Sangurima, who protect Los Rugeles (505). Patriarchal authority should never be contested in the *montuvio*'s world, and the one who cannot impose himself by violence is condemned to suffer the consequences.

Violence and "machismo" go hand in hand in this closed world. To conform to cultural and behavioral codes imposed by patriarchal power, apart from the household activities women have to bear children. They cannot participate in any decision making because their opinion does not count. Women have no "voice." Thus Ventura's wife has given birth to twenty-four children (478), and when Ventura warns his daughters against the Rugeles she cannot say a word: "Su mujer...se tragaba el llanto en un rincón" (504). When Ventura explains that he wants his daughters to finish school before getting married, Los Rugeles exclaim: "¿Pa qué mismo necesitan estudiar más? La mujer, con que sepa cocinar, a parir apriende sola..." (503). María Victoria who dares to break the pattern of submissiveness and silence and decides by herself dies the victim of Los Rugeles' vengeance. Thus she is punished for going against family norms and the patriarchal power structure is maintained. This low concept of women is consistent in every generation. The patriarch's third wife is secluded to one room of the house and thereby reaffirming the family space for women: "Vivía aún, inválida, chochando, encerrada en un cuarto de la casa grande de La Hondura (464). Thus although the narrator states that Nicasio "respects" his dead wives (465), the treatment he gives to the one who is still alive does not show such respect.

The only exception is Nicasio's mother, but there is a reason for it. She has extraordinary characteristics of courage, organization and self-determination. She succeeds in whatever she attempts to do. She even defies the patriarchal code and leaves her father's house in order to protect her illegitimate child, and she is not punished for her action. She escapes, establishes her small hut and starts to build up what under Nicasio's rule will become the biggest "latifundio" of the region. She is the real founder of La Hondura which will give power to the patriarch Nicasio. This is the reason for her being the exception and she lives only until her son is old enough to impose himself on others. Since among the *montuvios*, emotional life is centered around the mother though social respect is centered on the father (De la Cuadra, *El montuvio* 881), and since Nicasio's father is a foreigner, he bears his mother's last name. It is Nicasio's mother who established *La Hondura* but all her actions evolve around her son's needs. She is: "una amorosa garra que se le ajustaba al brazo, para llevarlo, sorteando los peligros, salvándolo y librándolo de todo" (474). Although proclaiming herself the owner of *La Hondura*, to secure power she has to recur to male legitimation. Thus she chooses the most powerful man among her "tenants" to be Nicasio's godfather (474). She does not have a "voice" in the text, when the action begins Nicasio is already an old man and it is only through his recollections that we learn about his mother. After her death Nicasio takes command of everything. Hence Nicasio and his mother are also the founding couple of this legendary place. This couple is "potentially incestuous" (Gilard, 76). As we shall see in the fourth chapter of this study, the machista attitude towards women will be critically revised by Yánez Cossío in *Bruna, soroche y los tíos*.

To survive, the enclosed world on *La Hondura* cannot have any outside interference. Thus when rumors of the crime committed by Los Rugeles reach Guayaquil, for the first time, the Rural Police enters *La Hondura* and imposes the law. After a terrible confrontation with Nicasio's group the authorities apprehend Los Rugeles (509-13).

There is an interesting innovation in the narrative technique in this part: the inclusion of newspaper articles from both the right and the left, condemning not only the barbarous crime but also the family system. The Sangurimas are seen as a family of maniacs and terrible exploiters. Their bloody history is exposed to the public (509).

Two elements have invaded *La Hondura*'s world and have disrupted it: exterior culture—Ventura's daughters whose values are no longer the same as those of the community—and military forces—the Rural Police looking for the criminals. In a world where the only law is the word of the patriarch, the arrival of exterior forces can not help but contribute to its destruction. There is no room for legend; the disaster arrives suddenly and destroys everything.

The epilogue, "Palo abajo," presents the patriarch in all his despair talking with Terencio, the priest, about his failed attempt to save Los Rugeles because Eufrasio did not cooperate:

> —El pendejo de Ufrasio dañó todito. Yo tenía otro plan... Pero Ufrasio no quiso... Nos habríamos acabado toditos... Claro; más mejor... **Más mejor que presos ellos y solo yo...**" (515, 516, emphasis added)

To lose his power before strange forces marks the collapse of Nicasio's world and his own way of life; this condemns him to a great solitude, and thus his last refuge is madness: "En los ojos alagartados de Don Nicasio la luz de la locura prendió otro fuego..." (516).

De la Cuadra creates an artistic work, a novel which portrays the Weltanschauung of the *montuvio*. The description of his way of life and the inclusion of his lexical expressions and diction make this character to enter the literary world. As Humberto Robles points out, in the subtitle "novela montuvia" De la Cuadra was already announcing that he was attempting a literary form whose paradigm was to be found in the narrative practices of the *montuvios* where there is coexistence of the imaginary, the real, the mythic, the hyperbolic, the grotesque. De la Cuadra explained those practices in his essay *El montuvio ecuatoriano*. The structural use of the "matapalo" to characterize the *montuvios* is an artistic discovery. He uses it not only to depict the mores of these people but also to denounce one of the major problems of the times, the "latifundistas." The image of the "matapalo," a tree that absorbs all that is nearby, is excellent for this purpose. The tree is also appropriate for describing the *montuvios'* life, which is socially centered around the father. Thus the first part of the book describes the *montuvios'* Weltanschauung and their mythical world centered around Nicasio, the master of the place. The reader's role is to understand the working of a different mentality.

In analyzing the discourse of *realismo maravilloso* in the first chapter, we noted the importance of the natural and supernatural or marvelous isotopies used to depict Latin American reality. Latin American writers have been concerned with similar themes for decades. When De la Cuadra wrote his novel, the "Discurso americanista" was at its heights. The ideology of this discourse is typical of the writers who make an effort to represent the totality of Latin American reality in fiction. "Arte de contenido y no arte por el arte" commented De la Cuadra about Ecuadorian literature of the 1930s, in his article "Feismo Realismo" (*Obras Completas* 973). In "Personajes en busca de autor" published in 1933 De la Cuadra advocates the need for writers to study their immediate reality, the local types, not in order to have a nationalistic literature but in order to find the universal:

> Siendo más regional se es más mundial, como siendo más inmediata-
> mente humano se es más universal...no es obra de romanos investigar
> en máquinas individuales conocidas y próximas...se corre el venturoso
> albur de topar—iminero feliz que encuentra la veta—con el momento
> anímico que resulte característico... Se dirá entonces... —He ahí algo
> tan humano que se ignoraba. Se lo descubrió registrando el espíritu
> de un indio de Sud América. (*Obras completas* 966, 967)

The same concern with the universal will be expressed years later by Alejo Carpentier in his well-known essay "Problemática de la novela latinoamericana:"

> No es pintando a un llanero venezolano, a un indio mejicano...como debe cumplir el novelista nuestro su tarea, sino mostrándonos lo que de universal, relacionado con el amplio mundo, pueda hallarse en las gentes nuestras—aunque la relación, en ciertos casos, pueda establecerse por las vías del contraste y las diferencias. (*Tientos y diferencias* 14)

In *Los Sagurimas* De la Cuadra is attempting to represent the marvelous American reality of the *montuvio*'s world and he succeeds in entering its different contexts including the mythical and the legendary. The *montuvios'* world is a cultural unity,[19] a reality. Violence, different laws, and the absence of taboos are part of that reality. De la Cuadra's use of humor and hyperbolic fantasy in this novel calls the reader's attention on what he is accustomed to find in contemporary works like *Cien años de soledad*.

As Octavio Paz in his essay "Spanish American Literature" says,

> Spanish American literature is not simply a body of works, but the relationship among these works. Each of them is a reply, spoken or silent, to another work written by a predecessor, a contemporary or an imaginary descendant. Our criticism should explore these contradictory relationships and show us how these mutually exclusive affirmations and negations are also in some sense complementary. (qtd. in González Echevarría, *The Voice of the Masters* 38)

Although readers are familiar with García Márquez's novel and probably have noticed its striking similarities to some of the facts referred to in *Los Sangurimas*, it is worth highlighting the following: the importance of the tree and incest; the homicide and exodus before the foundation of the place (in *Los Sangurimas*, Nicasio's father and also his uncle, and in *Cien años*, Prudencio Aguilar), the founding couple (Nicasio and his mother in La

---

[19]I am using this term in the sense described by Schneider: "A unit in a particular culture is simply anything that is culturally defined and distinguished as an entity. It may be a person, place, thing, feeling, state of affairs, sense of foreboding, fantasy, hallucination, hope, or idea. In American culture such units as uncle, town, blue (depressed), a mess, a hunch, the idea of progress, hope, and art are cultural units" (*American Kinship* 2). Umberto Eco proposes to use cultural unity instead of referent (*As formas do conteúdo* 15).

Hondura, José Arcadio and Ursula in Macondo). Both women founders show extraordinary personalities and abilities for organization. Both patriarchs are very old and at the end become mad. In both novels geographical location is extremely important, and there is a tree and a river (the river Mameyes and a carob tree in *La Hondura*, a river and a chestnut in *Macondo*). Both patriarchs plan and direct the construction of their houses; these are transformed according to the needs of the family, and there is plenty of light, sun and air. Love for solitude is the particular characteristic of Francisco Sangurima whose mysterious death is never clarified. Solitude is a constant in *Cien años*, and the death of José Arcadio is also an unresolved mystery. Colonel Eufrasio Sangurima participates in many revolutions, does not trust governmental politics, and has innumerable children by different women, the same characteristics that are well known in Colonel Aureliano Buendía. The drinking habits of Ventura and Terencio remind the reader of the parties given by Aureliano Segundo who imbibes and eats excessively. Nicasio's constant search for cultural identity is a well-known pattern in the characters of *Cien años*. There are other parallel details that may be easily observed after a close reading of both works, but there are many differences in the use of natural and supernatural elements. García Márquez is an expert in using both without transition. Of course, there exist many other contrasts in discursive strategies and narrative techniques since, after all, thirty-four years of fictional tradition have elapsed between the publication of both novels. Critics have noted the parallelism between *Cien años de soledad* and *Pedro Páramo* which was written twelve years earlier, pointing out the originality of the writers' vision of a magic Latin American reality rooted in a parallel attitude of the authors with respect to their cultural tradition. They have also noticed the similarities of both novels in the treatment of social and political problems common to the majority of the Latin American countries.[20] To call attention to similar elements in a Latin American novel published two decades earlier than Rulfo's work will help us to establish a literary tradition. As David William Foster says, "we must cease to devote all our critical energies to Gabriel García Márquez and Jorge Luis Borges and concern ourselves with the other vast literary riches of Latin America" (*Alternate Voices* xvi).

Commenting on De la Cuadra's work René de Costa asserts the following:

> Aunque el autor de *Los Sangurimas* no formuló una teoría, su obra narrativa demuestra hasta qué punto reconoció y aprovechó él mismo las posibilidades artísticas de su América ecuatorial. (52)

---

[20]See in this respect Suzanne Jill Levine's *El espejo hablado*, Chapter Two.

De Costa's affirmation is unquestionable, and what is important for our purposes is to stress the fact that these well-known and recognized elements of contemporary narrative were used artistically by José de la Cuadra in the early 1930s. Thus we can safely conclude that *Los Sangurimas* is a seminal work in the use of the amalgamation of the marvelous and the real as a new way of writing to expose social problems in Latin American fiction.

To exemplify the continuation of this new way of writing in the Ecuadorian novel of the 1970s we shall analyze in the next chapter two important works: Aguilera Malta's *Siete lunas y siete serpientes* and Yánez Cossío's *Bruna, soroche y los tíos*.

TWO ECUADORIAN NOVELS OF *REALISMO MARAVILLOSO* OF THE 1970s

> Para que un país tenga novela, hay que asistir a la labor de varios novelistas, en distinto escalafón de edades, empeñados en una labor paralela, semejante o antagónica, con un esfuerzo continuado y una constante experimentación de la técnica. (Alejo Carpentier, *Tientos y diferencias*)

The literary renovation reached by many Latin American countries during the 1950s and 1960s was not experienced in Ecuador where, during these years, there was a decline in literary production, especially in the novel. Agustín Cueva, in *Lecturas y rupturas*, explains the situation of the 1950s in Ecuador in these terms:

> Las razones de dicho declive son por supuesto múltiples, comenzando por el hecho más obvio: la realidad se modificó más rápido que la **Weltanschauung** de la generación del 30. Al entrar en una fase de franca desestructuración ("modernización" o modificaciones sectoriales) la vieja sociedad rural que fue el Ecuador se "descompuso," pero sin engendrar de inmediato una sociedad de nuevo tipo, plenamente urbana. En consecuencia, la concepción del mundo de los años treinta se marchitó antes de que surgiera una alternativa coherente para reemplazarla. El adocenamiento y el oportunismo hicieron el resto: desde la "gloriosa" del 44 hasta finales de los cincuenta el espíritu combativo de las capas medias decayó, fueron "cooptadas" como se diría hoy. (189)

During the sixties the cultural, political, and social issues in Latin America were also reflected in its literature. In Ecuador, there were changes in poetry, but there were no important novels to be equated to those of the great Latin American writers of the "boom," García Márquez, Cortázar, Fuentes, Vargas Llosa. This situation was to change, however, in the 1970s with the appearance of novels with as great a variety and richness of themes and complex narrative techniques as on the rest of the continent.

Some of the most important novels in the decade of the seventies are: Demetrio Aguilera Malta's *Siete lunas y siete serpientes* (1970), *El secuestro del general* (1973), *El jaguar* (1977); Alfredo Pareja Diezcanseco's *Las pequeñas estaturas* (1970), *La Manticora* (1974); Pedro Jorge Vera's *Tiempo de muñecos* (1971), *El pueblo soy yo* (1976); Alicia Yánez Cossío's *Bruna, soroche y los tíos* (1973), *Yo vendo unos ojos negros* (1979); Jorge Rivadeneira's *Las tierras del Nuaymás* (1975); Jorge Enrique Adoum's *Entre Marx y una mujer desnuda* (1976); Fernando Tinajero's *El desencuentro* (1976); Iván Egüez's *La Linares* (1976); ·Jorge Dávila Vázquez's *María Joaquina en la vida y en la muerte* (1976); Miguel Donoso Pareja's *Día tras día* (1976); Gustavo Alfredo Jácome's *Porqué se fueron las garzas* (1979) and Eliecer Cárdenas's *Polvo y ceniza* (1979). As Sacoto rightly states in *La nueva novela ecuatoriana*:

> La actual novela ecuatoriana, la de la década del 70, es bastante lograda en Hispanoamérica, advirtiendo, sin embargo, que no ha llegado a su cenit todavía y está muy lejos de su madurez. Algunos narradores ecuatorianos son muy jóvenes (Dávila, Egüez, Cárdenas) y están en período de gestación. En consecuencia, es mucho, pero mucho, lo que se puede esperar de la novela ecuatoriana, en los decenios a venir. (206)

For this study I have chosen two novels: Aguilera Malta's *Siete lunas y siete serpientes* (1970), and Yánez Cossío's *Bruna, soroche y los tíos* (1973); these works elucidate social problems of race, class and gender through use of marvelous realism.

Demetrio Aguilera Malta's *Siete lunas y siete serpientes*

> En esta obra voy a los mitos de mi infancia. El auto sacramental, el misterio. Se ha hecho una gran mutilación al prescindir de los mitos cristianos: ellos son para nosotros los más importantes. Jesús y el diablo. (Demetrio Aguilera Malta)

As mentioned in the third chapter, Demetrio Aguilera Malta was a member of the "Grupo de Guayaquil," and he contributed four short stories to the first publication of the group, a collected volume entitled *Los que se van* (1930). The setting of these stories is the coastal region of the gulf of Guayaquil, the same setting of *Don Goyo* (1933), *La isla virgen* (1942), and *Siete lunas y siete serpientes* (1970), Aguilera Malta's trilogy of novels of the tropics. Although all three present elements of *realismo maravilloso*, the third one marks a new stage in the writer's development. Here Aguilera Malta experiments with structure and language, situating this novel within the current trend of the new Latin American narrative. Since that year (1970) several Ecuadorian writers have followed his initiative.

Siete lunas y siete serpientes[1] denounces social exploitation, racial and class prejudices, religious decadence and general social problems, presenting them as the eternal question of good and evil. Although the above topics had already been treated in the social realism of the 1930s, the new approach of Aguilera Malta through incorporating another level of reality, that of myth and magic, allows the reader to see the complexity of social structure. The author no longer poses the old antinomy of "explotadores versus explotados" but instead puts forth a more elaborate and complete picture of social problems. He uses fragmentation of time, linguistic experimentation with Spanish, Latin and Quechua expressions, and cinematic techniques like foreshadowing, flashback and montage. A narrative voice gives account of the realistic marvelous attitude of the natives of a remote village, *Santorontón*, who believe in God, the devil, wizards, and in zoomorphic and magical transformations of the human being. These varied literary devices make the reading of *Siete lunas y siete serpientes* an exciting adventure into many cultural elements of the Latin American symbolic universe. The author, who is well versed in poetry, theater and cinematography, succeeds in presenting the reader with a "novela total" to which he is expressly committed.[2]

---

[1]Demetrio Aguilera Malta, *Siete lunas y siete serpientes* (México: Editorial Grijalbo, 1978). *Seven Serpents and Seven Moons*. Translated by Gregory Rabassa. Austin & London: Univ. of Texas Press, 1979. Quotations in the text correspond to these editions.

[2]"Creo en la novela total. Los ismos ya me tienen un poco fatigado. Pienso que al escribir una novela uno debe usar todas las técnicas a su alcance sin limitarse a una escuela particular. No creo que el autor debe ser un esclavo de las corrientes o modas literarias... En la novela es importante lo que se cuenta pero lo es también, principalmente, cómo se cuenta" (qtd. in Fama, "Entrevista" 18).

The plot develops in three geographical spaces: the center is *Santorontón*, a place where "what happens there doesn't happen"; Balumba, "the island of the wizard Bulu-Bulu;" and Daura, "the Quindales's little island." Throughout the novel, in characters and situations, the juxtaposition of good and evil and natural and supernatural elements has an important ideological and aesthetic function.

Among the forces of "good" are Father Cándido, the prototype of a Christian minister, whose main concern is to take care of the poor, the sick, and the oppressed; Juvencio Balda, the idealistic doctor who arrives in *Santorontón* at the highest moment of exploitation by the powerful; Clotilde Quindales, who was raped by Candelario Mariscal and who is the only survivor of the Quindales family; and Juan Isabel Lindajón, the poor man who lodges Balda at his arrival at *Santorontón*. Protecting this group, but only at critical moments, is a humanized Burned Christ, Father Cándido's "comrade."

The opposing band, that of the forces of evil, is constituted by the "mandamás de Santorontón" whose leader is Crisóstomo Chalena, the "water hoarder," who mercilessly exploits the poor; Salustiano Caldera, the Political Lieutenant; Rugel Banchaca, the chief of Rural Police; Father Gaudencio, the simoniacal priest, a partisan of the rich; Espurio Carranza, the "doctor-undertaker;" and Vigiliano Rufo, the storekeeper. With Chalena and his allies Aguilera Malta depicts the rich joining forces with the classic triumvirate of governmental, military and religious authorities who have dominated the life of many Latin American villages. We shall observe later the magical zoomorphic transformation of this group. Helping this group is the devil; however, according to a popular belief it is bad luck to name the devil as such. Thus throughout the narrative he is given at least fifteen different names: Old Longtail, The Malignant, The Seven Thousand Horns, The Green-Red-Soul-swallower, The One Whose Name is Never Spoken, and so on.

Candelario Mariscal and the wizard Bulu-Bulu are also among the characters who represent the forces of evil; however, they are somehow different from the rest, and they deserve special consideration. Candelario Mariscal, although evil in all his deeds and directly affiliated with the devil, does not care about money. He prevents Chalena (the richest man of the village) and his people from attacking Father Cándido's group while the latter are building the cistern. With this action Candelario is helping the poor because the water collected in the cistern will liberate them from Chalena's oppression. The wizard Bulu-Bulu and his family live isolated in their island, suffering from discrimination. Bulu-Bulu is not aligned with either group; he helps anybody, depending on circumstances.

As in all texts belonging to the category of new narrative in Latin America, temporal and spatial fragmentation are characteristic of this novel. It opens with Dominga, the wizard's daughter, in her seventh day of erotic obsession with the Tin-Tines and the snake, and Candelario Mariscal, on his way to see Bulu-Bulu, hoping to find a cure from the erotic persecution of the dead Chepa Quindales. It closes on the eve of his wedding with Dominga. Interwoven in this "time" are all the episodes corresponding to the development of *Santorontón* and various facts of the characters' life: Candelario's origins (17), his past bad deeds as Colonel (122-23), his attack on the Quindales (89-90); Chalena's past (46, 298-301), his establishment in *Santorontón* to exploit the poor, and his pact with the devil (79-85); the arrival of Juvencio Balda (174), his life as a medical student (229-37); the construction of the cistern where men and animals work together in "a kind of collective fever" (302); the story of Father Cándido (29), the Burned Christ (30-34, 66), and their continuous dialogues; the arrival of Father Gaudencio (192); the story of Bulu-Bulu, his origins (280-86), his magic powers, and so on. None of the episodes of the thirty-three chapters is narrated in logical sequence or with the same technique, nor do they have the same duration. Flashbacks and interior monologue are very common. Some of the important aspects we shall consider are: the juxtaposition of natural and supernatural codes without conflict, the ideologeme of "mestizaje," and the complex narrative technique and linguistic experimentation.

In *Siete lunas y siete serpientes* the coexistence of natural and supernatural elements without conflict, both forming a coherent and harmonious fictional reality, is a constant. This method is used to describe the magical world of the Santorontonians and also to criticize social and cultural problems. To achieve the presentation of a harmonious world, the narrator describes natural and supernatural events as if there were no difference in the perception of them. Since the natural and the supernatural are intrinsically interwoven in the fictitious world there is no hierarchy of reality. The narrator adopts the perspective of a community living in a world ruled by its own laws. The reader does not question but accepts this magical alien universe. In the microcosm of *Santorontón*, everything is possible. *Santorontón* is:

> un lugar donde las cosas empiezan a inventarse... Donde el Diablo aún baila en la punta del rabo. Donde el Hijo del Hombre no gana todavía sus últimas batallas. (317, 313)

The Burned Christ and the devil, protectors of the forces of good and evil, have human and supernatural characteristics. The Burned Christ gets down from his cross to rest when he is tired and comments to Father Cándido in a natural way, "¿Crees que no me canso de estar siempre clavado allá arriba?" (323). He uses his supernatural powers only at critical moments, the first time, when the Pirate Ogazno throws Father Cándido and the Crucifix into the sea; Christ and Cándido arrive safely at *Santorontón*, using the cross as a canoe.

This experience makes them "unos perfectos camaradas" (34). Later, when Candelario sets fire to the Church, Christ flies with Cándido far from the flames (61). In both cases the marvelous action does not disturb Cándido who accepts Christ's help as a natural consequence of their close relationship. Thus sometimes Cándido helps Jesus to carry the big cross across the jungle (322-23). Only once Christ exercises his supernatural powers in front of the community. In order to save Juvencio Balda from Chalena and the "mandamás," he descends from the cross and menaces the group with it (119). The characters see Christ's intervention as a normal fact. Chalena's people are frightened because they are caught in fault and they are going to be punished for their bad actions. For the "good" people, it is logical to receive help from Christ when they are in danger. Neither group marvels to see Christ alive, and most of the time his participation is as human as that of the other characters.

The devil is also described with human characteristics and Chalena, in the same way as Cándido with Christ, takes the devil's presence as something perfectly natural. The Santorontonians describe Old Longtail in this way:

> Aparecía generalmente en la alta noche. Nunca se quitaba el sombrero. Un sombrero negro. Pelado. Acaso sería para ocultar los cuernos. Asimismo, jamás se sentaba derecho. Como todos los cristianos. —¡Claro, él no era cristiano!— Más bien se ladeaba hacia la izquierda. Puede ser que a causa de la cola. Le estorbaría, sin duda. (18)

The narrative presents the people's perspective of the devil as the archetypal figure with horns and tail, but also endowed with supernatural powers to help his protegees; hence he makes rain fall only on Chalena's zinc roofs to help him to monopolize the water and sell it to the poor (87-88). According to the people's beliefs, he also helps Candelario in all his deeds, giving magical powers even to his "machete" which has a life of its own (107). There is no difference in the treatment of real and marvelous isotopies. In all descriptions realistic details are just as precise and convincing as that of the supernatural events. The supernatural appears as normal as the daily events of the Santorontonians' life.

Keeping the natural/supernatural juxtaposition, Christ and the devil each communicate directly with two characters in the novel: Christ with the two priests, Cándido and Gaudencio, and the devil with Candelario Mariscal and Crisóstomo Chalena. To reinforce the leitmotif of good and evil, there is a difference in the closeness of relationship with each character, depending on their behavior. With Cándido, the priest who protects the poor, Christ has a close relationship, for he is his constant companion, his "comrade." With Gaudencio, who favors the rich and powerful, Christ talks only twice: once when Gaudencio was helping Chalena and his group to get Juvencio Balda

(119), the "good" doctor, and then again towards the end of the novel, to dissuade Gaudencio from making his trip to Balumba (309).

Christ and Gaudencio discuss Candelario's faults. Soon from this individual case the discussion dialectically turns to religion and its true meaning. When Gaudencio defends the church as an institution that needs to maintain its power, Christ replies: "¿Crees que resulta mejor una Iglesia fuerte con una Religión débil? ¿O has llegado a la paradoja de una Iglesia sin Religión que la sustente?" (316). Gaudencio exemplifies not only the Church as the oppressive institution whose allies are the powerful but he is also the outsider, the colonizer. He is the European who has different values, who cannot understand either the local culture or the people's needs and who maintains an offensive "superior" attitude (193).

In a parallel way to Christ who is closer to Cándido, the good priest, the devil is closer to Chalena, who is worse than Candelario. Nonetheless the devil favors both with zoomorphic powers. Candelario becomes a caiman while Chalena becomes a frog. It is known that the crocodile came to signify fury and evil in the Egyptian hieroglyphics (Cirlot 67). These zoomorphic transformations serve a double purpose. On the one hand they make the reader enter the realm of myth and magic of the Latin American world. On the other hand, they are a writer's textual strategy for social criticism. Candelario Mariscal, besides being the image of gratuitous violence, so common in Latin America, helps the author to criticize institutionalized violence as well as to satirize military practices. Candelario stops in his crimes only because another more powerful appears, the "Ministro de Gobierno, Coronel Epifanio Moncada." According to Candelario the Minister does the job on a grand scale, "en forma legal y organizada. En un día entierra más gente que yo en un mes. No puedo atrevérmele" (131). Thus although Candelario by his own power became Colonel and made his helper Canchona, Captain (100-101), nevertheless he has to surrender to the higher authority. The devil favors Candelario's wickedness but he never talks directly to him, and Candelario does not call on him either. Christ comments that Candelario's faults are caused by an uncontrollable force, but because Candelario is open and does not have the passion for money "merece una oportunidad para su arrepentimiento y contrición" (317).

There is intertextuality at different levels in the figure of Candelario Mariscal. Prefiguration of this character can be traced to Aguilera Malta's own early writings, his short story "El cholo que se castró" (1930) and La isla virgen, 1942 (María E. Valverde, La narrativa 99). Two short stories of José de la Cuadra also come to mind "Banda de pueblo" (1932), where one of the characters is Severo Mariscal, a womanizer; and "Guasinton" (1938), whose protagonist is a fabulous caiman. Guasinton's extraordinary deeds are famous among the montuvios. Direct ancestors of Colonel Candelario Mariscal are

Colonel Eufrasio Sangurima (*Los Sangurimas*, 1934) and Colonel Aureliano Buendía (*Cien años de soledad*, 1967).

With Crisóstomo Chalena, the leader of the "Mandamás," the author treats the pact with the devil, a theme already used in literature in the past. In this text however, the pact exemplifies popular beliefs. We saw the same topic treated by De la Cuadra in *Los Sangurimas*, but while Nicasio never calls the devil, in Aguilera Malta's novel the devil is seen in action— Chalena calls the devil when he needs him. Nonetheless both writers are depicting the marvelous reality of the small villages of the Ecuadorian tropic.

Chalena's only ambition is money. He is the prototype of all the exploiters and tyrants whose cruelty and ambition have no measure; his metamorphosis when he commits evil acts is the symbol of his vileness. Chalena makes concessions to the powerful to get their cooperation; thus his allies are the "mandamás," the local authorities and important people of *Santorontón*.

In a parallel way to Christ who talks to Gaudencio about the problems of religion and the church in a universal dimension, the devil talks with Chalena regarding the poor. This conversation also takes on a universal dimension. Using the marvelous, the author criticizes many problems, especially the corruption of civil and religious authorities and the oligarchical structures that govern without ethical principles. The devil examines the widespread problem of poverty complaining to Chalena: "Por un lado, cada vez estoy más desprestigiado. Por otro, cada vez es mayor la competencia" (329). And by means of the capital sins he exposes the situation of the poor: poor people have nothing to be proud of; they don't have wealth left over to be avaricious; they don't have time or energy to look for lust; all are poor and have similar needs thus they cannot be envious of one another; since they don't have enough to eat, they cannot sin from gluttony; due to their poor condition they have to swallow their anger; and, finally, they cannot be lazy, for they have to work to survive (329-30). Chalena and his group are worse in their offenses than Candelario Mariscal. Clementine Rabassa properly states:

> Oligarchies are particularly susceptible to malversation and are prime material for anti-heroic characterization. In the scale of greater and lesser sinners which exist in the microcosm of *Siete lunas y siete serpientes*, the worst offenders are those who are supposedly serving the community but instead group together in a cohesive clique to oppress the villagers who depend on them. (*Social Justice* 149)

Aguilera Malta, rather than describing their baseness in a realistic way, uses the marvelous and transforms them into a three-headed serpent and five-headed crocodile. The distinctive use of the anaphora gives more force to the description:

Poco a poco, se fue integrando, en primer plano, la figura de una
víbora tricéfala. La cabeza del centro correspondía a Rugel Banchaca.
Las de los lados a los dos rurales. Atrás del ofidio de aspecto
tridente, daban vueltas cinco cabezas de caimán, sin cola. Cinco
cabezas de caimán unidas por el tronco... Cinco cabezas de caimán
horrible estrella viva de cinco puntas. Cinco cabezas de caimán que
eran las cinco cabezas humanas: Gaudencio, Chalena, Rufo, Caldera,
Carranza. (113-14)

With the figures of Christ and the devil, Aguilera Malta recreates the
"Auto-sacramental."[3] In the dialogues, morality is substituted by reflections on
social justice. The humanized Christ is a key figure; his discourse and actions
belong to this world. His preoccupation is to make humans realize their
limitations and wrongdoings. Christ does not make problems disappear
miraculously; poor people have to overcome many obstacles, and, although
towards the end there is some hope that things will get better, problems are
still there. Christ and the devil never confront each other, and they do not talk
to all the characters. They select carefully to whom and when they talk. In the
words of Christ to Gaudencio, the simoniacal priest, we can read the writer's
denunciation of social problems, oppression, racism, and discrimination.

This social concern is expressed in all of Aguilera Malta's narrative and
theater. Of particular interest is his drama *Infierno negro* (1967) where the
socio-political problems have also a universal dimension.[4] In *Siete lunas y
siete serpientes* the devil's discourse is written in an ironic humorous tone. Old
Longtail's problems are caused by changes in the behavior of young people
who no longer consider sins acts that were sins before (329). However,
embedded in the humorous expressions emerges the sad reality that the main
problem is caused by the increased number of indigent people who, due to
their poverty, cannot even commit capital sins.

---

[3]"Auto-sacramental" a one-act religious play dealing with the theme of the
Eucharist. "Autos sacramentales" were performed in the public squares of
Spanish towns on the afternoon of Corpus Christi Day during the 13th
through the 17th centuries. Symbolic and allegorical in character, they
comprised religious mythical and historical subjects (*Dictionary of Spanish
Literature*). For the development of the *auto sacramental* in Spain see
Alexander A. Parker's "Notes on the Religious Drama. . . ."

[4]For a detailed study of Aguilera Malta's theater see Gerardo A.
Luzuriaga's *Del realismo al expresionismo*.

By showing Christ and the devil interacting with men the message of the writer is explicit: human beings are responsible for social injustices, and it is here, on earth, that people must look for solutions to improve their situation. Latin American writers share similar concerns; we saw the same preoccupation in Carpentier's *El reino de este mundo*.

With Bulu-Bulu and his family the magic of the African and Indian world is introduced into the narrative, thus completing the elements which form part of the Latin American marvelous reality. For the Santorontonians, the belief in wizards and their magic powers is as important as their belief in God and the devil.

Aguilera Malta depicts popular beliefs as a natural integral part of the culture; thus the narrator describes Bulu-Bulu's magic powers from the Santorontonians' perspective. As a medicine man, Bulu-Bulu can heal all types of sicknesses, even "las enfermedades que no son de este mundo" (151). Most of the time Bulu-Bulu's actions are natural, the only time he appears with all his magical powers is when he goes to the jungle in the shape of a tiger. Bulu-Bulu Tiger disintegrates into parts in order to invite, at the same time, the wizards of ten generations to his daughter's wedding. The narrator describes Bulu-Bulu's transformation in short and rhythmical phrases as if nothing extraordinary has happened:

> Bulu-Bulu Tigre agitándose. Desprendiéndose. Dividiéndose. Bulu-Bulu Tigre y muchos... El Brujo en fragmentos. Bulu-Bulu brazos, Bulu-Bulu piernas. Bulu-Bulu rabo. Cabezas con ojos de fuego. Cuerpo brazos piernas orejas y rabo. De ébano y llama. (279)

Not only magic but also social and racial discrimination and slavery are introduced with Bulu-Bulu. The Santorontonians do not talk to Ña Crisanta after she marries Bulu-Bulu, for he is a wizard and also a black man (184-185). Ironically when people need treatment, they go to see Bulu-Bulu, and he does not discriminate.

Bulu-Bulu's arrival with the African slaves is described in this way:

> Antes—ese antes canoso cuatricentenario—él llegó en un barco negrero... Bulu-Bulu entre esclavos—príncipes, guerreros, vírgenes, artistas, artesanos, brujos—con cadena al cuello. Entre muchos esclavos. La mitad la devoró la distancia. La otra mitad, ¿estaba viva?... Las tripas resecas de hambre y de sed. Los cuerpos vestidos con huellas de látigo. Negrero. Empujados. Hundidos. Descendidos. Catarata de sangre y de lágrimas. (280)

Thus, although the description of racial prejudice and slavery is given a mythical dimension, it also reproduces the injustice of the situation. In

Ecuador the black population, together with the indigenous population, has been marginalized. As Oswaldo Díaz shows in his study *El negro y el indio en la sociedad ecuatoriana*, social relations between the black and the white population prove the existence of racism based on a power structure inherited since colonial times. This racism gains force and continues due to the ideology created by the dominant groups. Ecuadorian blacks are descendants from African slaves who survived the shipwrecks of slave-trading ships. These ships transported slaves from the "Virreinato de México" to the "Virreinato de Lima" (1553-1600) and frequently were destroyed due to the turbulent sea at San Francisco cape, now Republic of Ecuador (Díaz 14, 33).

The ideologeme of "mestizaje," the blend of different races and cultures, is also important in this novel. This issue has long been the preoccupation of Latin American writers but takes particular relevance in the twentieth century with the "discurso americanista." In *Siete lunas y siete serpientes*, "mestizaje" is treated throughout the novel, but it is demonstrated especially in the couples: Juvencio/Clotilde and Candelario/Dominga. With Juvencio and Clotilde besides racial and cultural "mestizaje," the theme of "civilización y barbarie" is given a new dimension because both the "civilized man" and the "primitive" community benefit each other.

Juvencio, who introduces modernity and progress to *Santorontón* by giving the Santorontonians the idea of starting a cistern to collect rain and thus avoid Chalena's abuse, gets the enthusiastic cooperation of the people. As in a return to the primal state of man living in harmony with the animal kingdom, in the construction of the cistern, all of the animals of the jungle come to help (303). This return to nature is possible thanks to Clotilde who had learned to communicate with the animals. Thus Clotilde is symbol of mother nature and Juvencio, who escaped from the problems of the city, will find peace only in contact with her.

Both Juvencio and Clotilde have psychological disorders which are presented through different types of discourse. Clotilde's problem is portrayed using the marvelous. Thus from being a victim of Candelario's violence—she witnessed Candelario's slaughter of her parents and was raped by him (92)—reversing the situation, in her imagination, she becomes the victimizer who avenges all women. Clotilde believed that she had sexual relations with all men who approached her and that afterwards she collected their testicles as a trophy. What she collected, in reality, were pine cones (153). Clotilde's obsession soon became a legend among the people, and her fame as the fascinating woman before whom all men surrendered extended in all the area: "Pronto la imaginación y la leyenda tejieron sus atarrayas de espuma. Una espuma que, como las pitahayas, tenía varias formas y colores" (93).

In contrast with Clotilde's obsession where the collective unconscious is at work—the Santorontonians propagated the legend—Juvencio's psychological disorder is not known. When he was in medical school, he experienced necrophilia. This episode is narrated in a long interior monologue by Juvencio as he discusses the water problem with Isabel Lindajón (229-30). By making Juvencio and Clotilde victims of psychological problems Aguilera Malta shows human nature exposed to tensions and problems in the city as well as in the country. Thus he once more breaches the gap between "civilización y barbarie." Towards the end of the novel Juvencio finds peace and is making plans with Clotilde to leave *Santorontón* and go to the city. *Santorontón* is changing; Balda can leave (369).

With the other couple, Candelario Mariscal/Dominga, two more myths are recreated: the return of the dead and the belief in magic powers and wizards who can cure or produce people's bewitchment. These beliefs form part of the native's culture. Dominga and Candelario are victims of singular erotic persecutions. Dominga is tormented by the Tin-Tines, legendary creatures who sexually persecuted women, and by a snake (9-16).[5] Candelario is persecuted by the ghost of Chepa Quindales. Bulu-Bulu wonders not about Chepa's return to the world of the living but about her sexual desire and exclaims: "Jamás oí que los difuntos tuvieran esas mañas" (76).

Clotilde's problem, although believed to be a reality by the Santorontonians, is explained in the narrative as a mental problem. Bulu-Bulu tells Candelario Mariscal that Clotilde's attacks on men were not true: "¡Todo era pura mentira!... ¿No le digo que andaba en la Luna?" (153). Her problem belongs to science; thus Bulu-Bulu sends her to a doctor in the city. Candelario's and Dominga's problem, however, belongs to the realm of myth and magic and is never doubted or discussed. Bulu-Bulu thinks that he is going to solve it by his performance of a rite of fertility for his daughter and a marriage "in Church," thus blending pagan and Christian elements.

---

[5]The Tin-Tines appear in previous works of Aguilera Malta. He refers to them several times in *Don Goyo* (1933) and in *La isla virgen* (1942). In the latter one of the characters describes them as follows:

> Dizque los mangles están llenos de Tin-Tines. Por las noches salen éstos a cazar las hembras de la costa, llenos de apetitos bestiales. Suben a las casas, adormecen a los hombres y cabalgan a las mujeres. Son pequeñitos, melenudos, con un cigarro enorme quemándoles la boca. Tienen la cabeza chata y grande. (*La isla virgen* 198).

Clementine Rabassa notes that "the belief that spirits or demons impregnated women is an ancient one and is noted in the magical texts of Babylonia of the Sassanian Era...The Tin-Tines of Ecuadorian folklore seem to function in a comparable manner as did certain Indo-Iranian deities" (*Social Justice* 129).

Dominga, the *montuvia*, bears Indian and Black blood and is the heir of the Christian and Indian myths and beliefs of her mother and the African rites of her father. The plot has an open-ended closure; thus it can be expected that after marrying Dominga, through love and repentance, the redemption of Candelario will be accomplished and *Santorontón* will have a new destiny, even if Chalena gets help from the devil. Colonel Candelario Mariscal is the only one who can oppose him.

Finally we have to consider the complex narrative technique. In order to convey all possible levels of reality Aguilera Malta uses different voices. He constantly intermingles description, dialogues and comments by a narrator with shifts in focalization. There is no chronological order for any of the events which are presented in a fragmentary way, starting "in medias res" or with flashbacks, after they have been accomplished. We can say that in this novel "temporal reference is deliberately sabotaged," to borrow Gérard Genette's words (*Narrative Discourse* 35). The last chapter epitomizes the techniques used in the novel. The order is the following: 1) A narrative voice informs the reader of Juvencio's thoughts and of his plans to leave *Santorontón* with Clotilde. 2) There is a dialogue between Juvencio and Clotilde with comments by a narrator. 3) A shift in focalization to Chalena occurs. The narrator informs the reader not only of Chalena's state of mind in the present—when he is happy about his new pact with the devil where he asked not for money but for crosses—but also of his bad past experience and his first pact when he sold the devil his soul for money. 4) Conversations among Chalena, Rugel and Salustiano, appear with comments by a narrator. Chalena informs his men that Candanga will help him in his plans. 5) There is a shift in focalization from Chalena to Christ and Father Cándido with dialogue between them and comments by the narrator. 6) Christ tries to convince Cándido that he has to go to the wedding. 7) The voice of Candelario is heard calling "Godfather," and Cándido answers: "I'm coming." 8) The dialogue between Christ and Cándido continues. Cándido is finally convinced by Christ to change his clothes to go to the wedding.

Throughout the plot when the narrator conveys the Santorontonians' perspective, where real, mythical, and imaginary reality are but one, there is never doubt or astonishment before the marvelous. The Santorontonians are absolutely convinced of their beliefs, of their world. However, there are moments of doubt in the narrative. These doubts are expressed only by the outsiders who do not have the same world view as the Santorontonians.

For example, the two priests' doubts are expressed sometimes in free indirect discourse, as in the third chapter. When Cándido hears the voice of Christ he thinks: "¿Sueño? ¿Realidad?" (26). Further, using a conventional third person narrator Aguilera Malta writes: "A veces, el cura dudaba. ¿No llevaría adentro al Nazareno?" (34). Gaudencio, after his experience on his trip to Balumba, thinks: "¿Habría soñado?" (318). These authorial interventions give force to the critical reading. The reader is called back to the "realidad total." They help to capture the reality of the Santorontonians and that of the outsiders who have different values.

A similar technique was observed in the novels analyzed in the second chapter of this study. In *El reino de este mundo*, Mackandal's flight is described presenting two points of view: that of the slaves and that of the colonists. In *Cien años de soledad*, the assumption of Remedios the Beauty is believed only by the inhabitants of *Macondo*, not by the foreigners.

The text ends on the eve of Candelario and Dominga's wedding for which the reader has been waiting from the beginning and which never takes place. By the same token, only in the last chapter of the novel the reader knows for sure that Chalena, in fact, made a pact with the devil, although the Santorontonians have already commented on this episode several times. These different shifts in focalization make the reader more conscious of the problematic world described.

There are other techniques, such as facts being recounted in flashbacks or through interior monologues, or the same fact being narrated from different perspectives. Candelario's story with La Chepa starts through his confession to Bulu-Bulu with flashbacks and different comments by the narrator; the problems of Juvencio and Clotilde are presented via interior monologues. But Clotilde's story is not only narrated through her interior monologue. Bulu-Bulu tells it to Candelario, Juan Isabel Lindajón, and Juvencio Balda. In addition, the Santorontonians relate imaginary encounters with her, thus creating the legend.

A similar technique is applied to develop the legend of Candelario's cruelty. His fearsome image grows and changes according to the imagination of the Santorontonians who keep adding details of his wrongdoings and most of the time give him the attributes of The Evil One, thus making it impossible to oppose his powers.

Another important aspect of this novel is linguistic experimentation which contributes to the sense of *realismo maravilloso*. Linguistic experimentation is a characteristic of all modern narratives, but magico-realistic writers use it with a serious purpose, and ludic playfulness is intended to send a specific message. In *Siete lunas y siete serpientes*, the varied utilization of language is perhaps Aguilera Malta's most important accomplishment. Forging his own style through expressions in Quechua, Latin, and Spanish, plus linguistic innovation, accumulations of images, and similes and metaphors, the author succeeds in presenting the complex reality of *Santorontón*, a reality that well could be applied to any other remote village in Latin America.

Here the author comments on his use of Quechua, Latin and Spanish:

Busco el quichua como valor semántico, sintáctico. Pero también
onírico. Hay una onomatopeya lejana de ancestro africano. Esto es
lo lejano. Lo cercano, la vertebración castellana con los elementos
fonales de dos lenguas, el quichua y el latín. (qtd. in Rodríguez
Castelo "Demetrio Aguilera M." 29)

Chalena's greediness is expressed in his metamorphosis by playing with
Quechuan words, and thus Chalena becomes a toad, small, big, green, black,
yellow. The Quechua and Spanish words convey his subhuman state:

Sa-u. Po-cug. Sapo-ucug. Sapo verde. Sapo negro. Sapo amarillo.
Sapo hinchado. No sapo chico-jambatu. Sapo grande-ucug... El sapo
Chalena. Chalena no jambatu. Chaluna ucug. ¿Rurruillag Chalena?
¿Chalena capón? ¿Rurruillag Ucug? (255)

Latin and Quechua are used in Juvencio's interior monologue which
conveys his mental state:

¿La Luna **sapientum**? ¿La ciudad entera musácea paradisiaca
sapientum? En represalia, serpentinas de bilis. Bilis estela largo hilo
de rabia telaraña de frío verde chiri lumar. ¡Achachay! Huagllichina.
Huagllichigrina. Huagllichicuna Huallichimuna. (237)

In all of the descriptions one discovers not only one aspect of language
but a combination of elements: images, repetitions, alliteration, metonymy,
synecdoche, playfulness of names. Poetically short and rhythmical phrases plus
repetition create descriptions that are characteristic of "enchantment," which
can be observed in any of the chapters no matter what subject is described.
This is Bulu-Bulu's announcement of his daughter's wedding:

Una noche, se fue Bulu-Bulu—el primero y el último, y el mismo de
siempre—. Caminó hasta la orgía vegetal Bulu-Bulu... Bulu-Bulu que
estaba de boda. Bulu-Bulu que casaba a su hija Dominga en
Balumba. Que seguía enhebrando el aviso en la aguja viajera del
viento. "Hay boda en Balumba." Bálumba-Balumba. Balumba-
Balumbá. (286)

This is the description of Candelario's transformation the night he attacks
the Quindales:

La sangre se enciende. Caymantapachaca manajaycapi canta. El puñal
en las fauces... El puñal de marfil. —Redoma del viento. Remolino
del iris. Imanes del sexo. —La lengua de vidrio. La sangre de humo.

La voz de metal. Candelario. Candela-río. Mar-iscal. Candela-río. Candela-mar. (67)

In the first description the enchanting and rhythmical phrases render the emotion experienced by Bulu-Bulu, the father, who is going to liberate his daughter from the Tin-Tines. In the second, the enchanting phrases are more forceful in the condemnation of Candelario's crime than ordinary words.

Referring to Cabrera Infante's *Tres tristes tigres* Haroldo de Campos in his essay "Superación de los lenguajes exclusivos" states that the "**féerie** verbal (unida a los montajes de palabras de **Altazor** de Huidrobo y al 'glíglico' de ciertos pasajes de Cortázar) parece desmentir la incredulidad borgeana sobre las tendencias lúdicas del idioma castellano" (295). The same could be applied to Aguilera Malta's writing. But it could also be added that Aguilera Malta forges his language to convey the "realidad total" and gives the reader the magic, the marvelous as well as the problematic aspects of the Santorontonians' world:

> Para mí hay una sola realidad. Lo que ocurre es que lo objetivo, lo concreto, lo inmediato es solo una parte de ella. La realidad es lo que captan mis sentidos, pero también es lo que imagino y lo que sueño. Es decir que, para mí, no hay una oposición entre realismo, surrealismo, realismo mágico o cualquier otra clase de realismo sino que todas estas realidades parciales son partes integrantes de una misma realidad total. (Fama, "Entrevista" 18)

Fama remarks accurately:

> En *Siete lunas y siete serpientes* el lenguaje se aparta de su tradicional sentido gramatical y se adecúa al ambiente primitivo y mágico. El sentido de las palabras se encuentra en la intuición que comunican y en la sensación que crean. (*Realismo mágico* 128)

Aguilera Malta uses repetition and alliteration, and he forms words by adding syllables or decomposes words by suppressing parts of them, as in the following phrases: "San. Santo. Santoron. Santorontón" (91), "Alas de atarraya atarrayán atarrayando. Candil candilón encandilando. Y ahora bajo el sol solán solando" (102), "Los ojos-ojillos, ojales, ojículos" (134), "Chalena-sapo sapón sapete-estaba triste tristón tristete" (327).

In the poetic prose of Aguilera Malta, there are many images and metaphors with connotations that make the reader enter immediately into the magical world of *realismo maravilloso*. These are a few examples: In the fights instigated by Old Longtail, "el acero fustigaba a la noche con latigazos de luz" (18). When Candelario attacks the Quindales: "La noche de los Quindales llovía lujuria en el mar y en las montañas" (67). The poor women undressed before Chalena are "—eclosión de carne morena—a la óptica voracidad impotente" (148). Juvencio Balda is "fabricante de fantasmas" (227) or, "farol vivo de esquina atornillado a las distancias insalvables" (231). Clotilde is "vivo imán de carne" (93), her hands are "mariposas de fuego" (89), and she is dressed "de caricias soñadas" (181). Candelario is "Fuego-agua. Sexo-sangre. Hombre-saurio" (67). La Chepa Quindales is "Difunta en llamas" (363). "¡Muerta-argolla! ¡Muerta-cadena! ¡Muerta-imán!" (156). Dominga is "sexo-imán" (72). Ña Crisanta is "racimo erecto de plátanos enjutos" (17). Chalena, besides being a frog, is "araña monstruosa" (112), "víbora invisible" (178), "paleta cromática" (179). The ship's sails are "murciélagos grises" (286), impatience is "brasero bramante" (45), and the sun is "erizo de coral" (53).

In summary, through his version of *realismo maravilloso*, Aguilera Malta's artistic work sheds light on different aspects of Latin American reality. It shows the abuse of power, the corruption of civil and religious institutions, the problems of social and racial discrimination, and the different elements of Latin American "mestizaje" where Christian, Indian, and African traditions intermingle. A world where the coexistence of "civilización" and primitivism is possible. In the "discurso americanista" the ideologeme of "mestizaje" is a positive hope for a better future. With this work Aguilera Malta gives us, through literature, the same positive message. With the couples Juvencio/Clotilde and Candelario/Dominga, where racial and cultural "mestizaje" are the elements that finally will change *Santorontón* despite its problems, the author gives a message of hope and faith in "mestizaje."

An artistic work has been accomplished in the terms of Ramón Xirau:

> Arte que no se contenta con describir la realidad sino que busca, más allá de los hechos y las costumbres—y muchas veces haciéndonos ver más claramente costumbres y hechos; siempre sin abandonar la realidad de donde el arte nace—el fundamento de unos y otras. (203)

Alicia Yánez Cossío's *Bruna, soroche y los tíos*

> She had been getting ready for her great journey to the horizons in search of *people*; it was important to all the world that she should find them and they find her. (Zora Neale Hurston, *Their Eyes Were Watching God*)

Alicia Yánez Cossío is considered by many as Ecuador's leading woman writer. She has published three books of poetry: *Luciolas* (1949), *De la sangre y el tiempo* (1964) and *Poesía* (1974), a collection of short stories: *El beso y otras fricciones* (1975) and five novels: *Bruna, soroche y los tíos*, which won the Ecuadorian National Prize in 1972, *Yo vendo unos ojos negros* (1979), *Más allá de las islas* (1980), *La cofradía del mullo del vestido de La Virgen Pipona* (1985), and *La casa del sano placer* (1989).

Bruna, soroche y los tíos[6] tells the story of Bruna and her family. Through Bruna's experience and using *realismo maravilloso* Yánez Cossío also makes a critical and dialectical review of the condition of Latin American society in general and the social role of women, in particular. This is important for, as we shall see, Yánez Cossío makes her reviews from a feminist point of view which contrasts with the traditional role generally attributed to women in all the novels we have analyzed here, particularly *Los Sangurimas* and *Cien años de soledad*.

Yánez Cossío treats different social problems as cultural myths using elements of marvelous realism. "Myth is a system of communication, that is, a message," writes Roland Barthes in his *Mythologies* (109). That is quite true in this novel. Bruna's family is a microcosm of society and the author uses the marvelous to offer a strong critique of it. When analyzing the text it is important to consider the two lexical meanings of "marvelous": (1) "unusual, extraordinary"; and (2) "supernatural, magic." The juxtaposition of natural and marvelous—"supernatural"—events occurs in reference to the Indian María Illacatu. In the other cases there is a juxtaposition of natural and marvelous—"unusual"—elements.

The title itself is a synthesis of its social context: *Bruna, soroche y los tíos*. First, Bruna is not the protagonist. Instead she acts as the intermediary of the different epochs by remembering episodes of the family history that she has read or has witnessed, or that Mama Chana, the old servant of the family, has told her. Through Bruna's memories, the woman emerges as a kind of mosaic whose different characteristics are depicted in each of the nine female characters of the novel. The social condition of women shows little change from the colonial times to the present. Thus there is a constant fragmentation only in "time" as traced by Western ways. Time as accounted by generations showing the social condition of women is relatively "continuous." Which is another contrast Yánez Cossío makes and adds to Bruna's truth, rebellion and success. The repetition of different social circumstances for men and women throughout six generations recreates "the woman's place," one of the myths which Yánez Cossío denounces. This condition transcends time.

---

[6]Alicia Yánez Cossío, *Bruna, soroche y los tíos* (Bogotá, Ediciones Paulinas, 1974). Quotations in the text correspond to this edition.

Second, *soroche* is the illness of the city. Soroche refers in everyday language to the difficulty of breathing people experience in some high places due to the rarefaction of the air.[7] In the novel it has a structural function; it represents the variety of prejudices, ignorance, and restrictive rules of a society where families pay tribute to *honra*, class and race. In this social context, moreover, physical work is regarded with contempt, and fear of criticism and obsession with religion are the norm. The concepts of *honra* and *honor* played an important role in Spanish literature in the XV and XVI and XVII centuries. At that time *honra* was understood as the *opinión* that others expressed about an individual. The opinion of the community was crucial not only in the public but also in the private life of individuals (Américo Castro, *De la edad conflictiva* 66-78). Yánez Cossío refers to *honra* when criticizing the mores of the city.

Third, "Los tíos," Bruna's "uncles," are her grandfather's cousins. They set the old and incredible ambience of the "ciudad dormida" (sleeping town) where the marvelous seems to be an everyday event.

The novel opens and concludes with brief sections (in italics) with the focalization on Bruna, far away from her town and free from the "soroche." In the rest of the text (thirty-three numbered chapters) the focalization shifts to specific facts in the life of different members of the family. These episodes affect not only the characters involved but also the life of the entire family and consequently, the life of the city. From Bruna's hotel window, the narrative moves to the house of the "tíos." This juxtaposition hotel-house is important because of its implications: what is transient, nonpermanent by contrast to what is stable, permanent. In Bruna's case, because she is a female, it also represents freedom in contrast to oppression. Most of the marvelous events that are to emerge in the central chapters are anticipated in this introduction (the sighs of María Illacatu, the bishop and his two hundred and forty-five sons, the marvelous rug of Alvarito Catevil, and Camelia Llorosa and her court of admirers). With the focalization on Bruna at the beginning and at the end, the story closes its circular movement. The structure emphasizes the long and overwhelming conditions of the city under the magic of "soroche" and the need Bruna had to escape from it.

The stagnation of the "ciudad dormida" is masterfully conveyed through fragmentation of time, juxtaposition of different historical periods which are recognizable from the facts recounted in the novel. It is possible to consider that time elapses from the seventeenth to the twentieth centuries. The length of time passed is reinforced by the only specific date given, 1743, the year of the dedication of the monument to the Bishop Salomón de Villacato, Bruna's

---

[7]See *Diccionario ideológico de la lengua española*; 2a ed.

grandfather (101), who was still alive when the monument was erected. In Bruna's time, who lives in the twentieth century, the mores of the city are still the same as in the eighteenth century. People still live under social and religious rigid laws. Dramatizing the indifference of people and their attachment to the old customs the narrator states that "el tiempo había hecho una estación definitiva en la ciudad, parecía no correr, hecho un nudo ciego" (48).

Six generations are represented through the characters of this novel. Their chronology follows:

Besides the immediate family three other women are mentioned: "la viuda del hijo mayor" (the oldest son's widow); Milka (Gabriel's wife) and Mama Chana, the family servant. Major differences between male and female social roles and status are brought into relief through these characters.

Gender differences appear from the beginning. Men are more educated than women. There is a clear division of labor within which men are in charge of the "valued," "honorable" and "respected" roles and women are systemati- cally relegated to the house. Maternity, virginity, and the different myths created by society are presented as valuable and desirable in women. The text presents the saga of the Latin American woman of the Andean region from the Spanish Conquest to modern times. Woman appears only in her "classic" roles of mother, widow, nun, or spinster. It is Bruna who finally breaks this pattern.

Besides gender differences, Yánez Cossío brings to bear issues of class and race, a preoccupation she shares with other Latin American writers such as Rosario Castellanos.[8] In countries of the Andean region and Mexico because there still exist large Indian populations, class and race constitute a central problematic. In Bruna's family two cultures are confronted, the Spanish and the Indian. One of the main accomplishments of Yánez Cossío is the characterization of the Indian woman and the portrayal of her suffering, frustrations, and humiliations before the Spanish conquerors. All of the Indian women's stories are captured in María Illacatu's story. The author uses the marvelous to portray the social situation, the Indian context in this case. She incorporates the importance of myth, magic, the identification with nature and the supernatural powers that the Indians attribute to it. They call nature "Madre-Tierra" (Motherland) and refer to it as the source of life. This use of marvelous and mythical elements which refer to Latin American reality is typical of the discourse of marvelous realism.

First generation. María Illacatu is the daughter of a rich "cacique" (Indian chief), and when the Spanish adventurer takes her, there is an eclipse, and she leaves her soul in the highest tree of her land:

> El cacique tenía una hija que sería la esposa del sol. Pero cuando los aventureros la encontraron, el sol se eclipsó y María Illacatu dejó su alma prendida en la punta del árbol más alto. (30)

The woman is torn away from her land, her family, and her "Indian" identity. Even her name is taken away: "yo te bautizo, Yahuma, con el nombre de María" (24). This renaming of the Indian is the first violent imposition of the foreign culture in her life, "to a new situation corresponds a new name" (Lotman 128). Derrida in *De la Grammatologie* (164) emphasizes the violence implied in the act of naming. Using the marvelous Yánez Cossío shows how the young native woman suffers in silence, communicates her feelings to nature, and nature responds to her:

> Contó el secreto de su maternidad al camino y el camino se apiadó de ella cortándose de repente... [L]a tierra se corrió a las quebradas y las montañas se retiraron. El camino se contrajo: diez árboles entraron dentro de uno. Los pájaros cayeron muertos de vejez y los huevos acabados de poner, se hicieron alas. (31)

---

[8]See Castellanos' *Balún Canán* (1957) and *Oficio de tinieblas* (1962).

This description from the Indian's perspective is done with assertiveness, it avoids the "unusual" and instead gives the narrative a tone of enchantment. Yahuma's suffering and dispossession and her transformation into María Illacatu is captured in the description of a portrait made by a local painter. The artist paints Yahuma in all her beauty but with a clear skin color to please social conventions:

> Quien hizo el cuadro, la pintó tal como era. Pero, influido por los convencionalismos de la época, le quitó la piel que tenía, y así desollada, la puso en carne viva la piel que le prestó el marido para que posara. María Illacatu perdió la piel cobriza en el lienzo con el mismo estoicismo con que perdió su razón de existir. (26-27)

"Re-naming" and "re-painting," are the first steps towards an effacement of the "cultural identity" which Bruna will search and recuperate. María Illacatu's revenge is silence. She understands the language of the conqueror but refuses to speak it even in crucial moments. Silence is her rebellion against the culture the Spanish want to impose by eliminating her own. Silence is María Illacatu's "space of resistance" (Ludmer, "Tretas del débil"). It also suggests a lack of communication whose consequence is solitude. Both are central themes in the novel. There is lack of communication between men and women and among generations. Silence is graphically represented in Maria Illacatu's dialogue with her husband, after his return from Spain where he has left her children to be educated:

> —¿...?
> —Los dejé allá, en España.
> —¿...?
> —A que se eduquen.
> —¡...! (34)

Since the only function allowed to this woman is maternity, once the children are grown up, the husband decides to send the children abroad and abandon her, but María Illacatu cannot suffer the separation from her children. Thus she decides to take justice into her own hands and reversing the situation, from victim she becomes victimizer. One night when her husband returns home she kills him, but it is not a simple killing, it is mediated by a marvelous sequence of events:

> Abrió por primera vez un costurero...y sacando unas afiladas tijeras las clavó en el corazón del hombre... Las tijeras se quedaron por un momento fijas al sentir el calor de la sangre: experimentaron el placer de penetrar en un ser tibio, húmedo, y con movimiento, y

luego, borrachas de placer y de lujuria, comenzaron por su cuenta a cortar y cortar el cuerpo tendido... María Illacatu se lavó las manos tintas en sangre, lentamente comenzó a destrenzarse y...se ahorcó con su propio cabello... (34-35)

In the above paragraphs there is no difference in the treatment of the real and marvelous isotopies. The marvelous action of the scissors follows naturally María Illacatu's action. The scissors continue on their own tearing to pieces her husband's body while María Illacatu washes her hands and slowly starts to unbraid her hair in order to hang herself with it. To terminate her life could seem to be a tragic end; death, however, in the Indian tradition means the continuation of life in a different way, thus a liberation, a "new life." Life which is always growing, repeating its vital cycle (Moreno 197-98).

María Illacatu is a victim of double discrimination: as a woman her role is only to have children; as an Indian, she is considered good for her inheritance of gold and precious stones, so much cherished by the Spaniards. Motherhood will be the role of women, and male domination from generation to generation will be represented in the narrative to show how society creates the "woman's situation." Yánez Cossío as many other modern women writers successfully conveys through strategies of representation the same plight of woman denounced by Simone de Beauvoir in 1949 in *Le Deuxième Sexe*: "On ne naît pas femme: on le devient."[9]

Second generation. The widow of the oldest son, who has no name, represents widows in general and shares the conditions of women who have neither education nor rights and whose duties are restricted to raising children and to taking care of the house:[10]

---

[9]Rosario Castellanos in *Mujer que sabe latín* (1973), acknowledges de Beauvoir's statements and tells us:

A lo largo de la historia (la historia es el archivo de los hechos cumplidos por el hombre y todo lo que queda fuera de él pertenece al reino de la conjetura, de la fábula, de la leyenda, de la mentira) la mujer ha sido más que un fenómeno de la naturaleza, más que un componente de la sociedad, más que una criatura humana, un mito. (7)

[10]Several studies have been done which discuss the role of woman in society, questioning her "natural" association with the domestic world and with a lower order of culture than men. Of particular interest on this subject are Sherry B. Ortner's article "Is Female to Male As Nature Is to Culture?" and Michelle Zimbalist Rosaldo's "Woman, Culture, and Society: A Theoretical Overview."

> Las mujeres no tenían ningún tipo de instrucción, no se les permitía
> ni hojear un libro por temor de que se hicieran hombrunas. Sólo
> podían tener contacto con la aguja, la escoba y las ollas. (54)

Third generation. Carmela, the oldest daughter of "el hijo mayor" is an exceptional case. Her story differs from the rest of the family because she is the first who has the opportunity to leave the "ciudad dormida" and is able to live, while abroad, free from "soroche." In Carmela's story the cultural myth of virginity the "warranty patent" indispensable for the marriage of women in traditional societies is treated extensively.[11] At the age of fifteen she has to travel to Spain to marry an old and noble man. In this marriage, nobility is as important to Carmela's family as her fortune is to the Spaniard; such marriages were often arranged during colonial times. During the trip, the protection of Carmela's virginity is the main concern because it constitutes the "honra" of the family name and thus guarantees a convenient marriage. When Carmela arrives the old man is already dead and she passes from adolescence to widowhood without having ever been married (61-65). When she returns to "la ciudad dormida," people question her virginity because she is different from the other women: she smokes, has many admirers, and conducts at her house a literary salon in the style of the Parisian salons of the eighteenth century. After a late marriage she abandons her impotent husband and enters a convent, which she has to leave to take care of her sister's children Catalina, Clarita and Francisco (65-85). Thus even this "liberated" woman ends "fulfilling" her female role, as do the rest of the women in the family. Catalina, Clarita and Francisco are the three "tíos" Bruna will visit every Thursday. They are not the sisters and brother of Bruna's parents, but cousins of her grandfather whose monument was erected in the eighteenth century. This anachronism gives an account of the old fashioned city whose way of life is two centuries behind the times and where "soroche" affects everybody. The noble, liberated Carmela becomes one more victim. She, as the rest of the women in town, has to comply with the demands of society.

Through two opposite stereotypes of spinsters are represented the women of the fourth generation. Catalina, the typical "beata," full of prejudices whose only obsession is to gain indulgences for the souls in Purgatory (150-53). She hates children (152) and has always opposed her sister Clarita's suitors (203). By contrast, Clarita loves life, children, and cats (201). The opposite personalities of Catalina and Clarita make any communication between them impossible. The gender contrast is established with "tío Francisco" who, as a man, has special privileges.

---

[11]Carmen Naranjo in *Mujer y cultura* discusses several of the cultural myths imposed on women by society.

Among the "tíos" the marvelous is used to single out the futility of their lives, each devoted to a different obsession. Catalina is extraordinary due to her unusual behavior. Clarita and Francisco incorporate supernatural elements. Thus the two meanings of marvelous (extraordinary and supernatural) are present. In Catalina, the absurd preoccupation with religion becomes so unusual that it soon gains marvelous proportions. To count indulgences she hires an accountant and buys an adding machine. Everybody in town comes to see the "machine for indulgences" (160). In Clarita's case, the cats also function as a marvelous thing for the whole system developed by her to raise them is beyond the natural and ordinary; as well, in her last days she pays rent to the phantoms who had invaded the house (200). She represents the weak woman unable to break family pressures, thus, to overcome her frustrations she centers her life around cats. As for "tío Francisco," his obsession with match boxes disturbs the harmony of the family, to the point that he continues with his collection and interacting with people even after his death. His privilege is to be a man (117-23).

In the fifth generation, María 23, daughter of the famous bishop of the city, is another victim of the gender differences already established: her two hundred and forty-five brothers are educated by the bishop himself; she is sent to the country without any education (109). Due to the number of children and for disciplinary reasons each child had a Christian name and a corresponding number according to their order by birth. Here again, the marvelous (unusual) is used by Yánez Cossío, but she uses it ironically: innumerable are the rules imposed on society by religious authorities. On the other hand, the numbers given to the children represent an impersonal way of dealing with children, which leads into the twentieth century and perhaps contributes to Bruna's independent point of view. Her family is the stereotype of the modern nuclear family characterized by high mobility. María 23 and her husband live in the country far from the "soroche" and start a family only when they come to the city (113). Of all their children, we know only Bruna and Gabriel who represent the sixth generation.

Bruna rebels against the customs of the town. She symbolizes the triumph of "mestizaje," the blend of different elements without contradiction and she is also the character that questions the establishment. While her aunts are afraid of revealing their Indian roots, for Bruna, the discovery of her Indian ancestor María Illacatu is the reaffirmation of herself. Before she was "un ser en el aire" (26), but when she starts using her Indian surname everything changes:

> Desde que escribió junto a su nombre el apellido que en realidad le correspondía, sintió que sus pisadas en el mundo tenían más firmeza. (26)

Bruna, much to the dismay of her relatives, decides to acknowledge her Indian ancestry; in reclaiming it she finds the power to claim her gender rights. In the classist and patriarchal society of "la ciudad dormida" where women and Indians are marginalized, Bruna's attitude of acknowledging her Indian ancestor addresses and revaluates both the importance of woman and that of the Indian roots. These two factors constitute the basis for Bruna's stability. Her adoption of the Indian name denotes the revalorization of the Indian values characteristic of the ideologeme of "mestizaje" in the 20th century. Considering the restricted ambience where she lives this is a daring act. Bruna is also the first to break with the classic cult to the elders, and she is not afraid of judging them according to their acts: "¿Mi tío abuelo? ¿El loco de los fósforos?" (21). Yánez Cossío often criticizes family institutions.

Different education for men and women persists even in this generation. Bruna is only a secretary and has to stay in town; Gabriel is sent to study engineering in Paris. Resenting this difference Bruna complains. She knows that the myth of virginity that prevails in the city is the main reason why she cannot travel abroad:

> Un chico puede ir a París, o al fin del mundo. No tiene una virginidad que cuidar, ha nacido con el privilegio de ser hombre. Mientras ella no puede ir sola del colegio a la casa que dista pocas cuadras. Ha nacido con el estigma de ser mujer, está condenada al "ghetto". (169)

In this generation other truths also come to light through secondary female characters. A significant role in Bruna's life is played by Milka, her sister-in-law. Although this character is not well developed, she is important because of the impact she has on Bruna. Milka is a dancer Gabriel meets in Paris and for whom he abandons his studies (170). She is a foreigner; thus she does not have any of the inhibitions given by the "soroche." She arrives with Gabriel one day and stays with the family overnight. In this short time, she gives Bruna a gift to share with her friends, special bathing suits which, once in the water, dissolve. Bruna gives these to her classmates, without knowing the consequences (230). As a result, her classmates stay seventy-two hours in the water. They prefer to get pneumonia than to leave the swimming pool naked; again, irony and exaggeration are used to ridicule sexual repression. Bruna's best friend dies after this experience and the whole city turns against Bruna for her action (232). Bruna cannot bear this last trial and decides to leave the city, following the same route of her grandfather with the hope to meet Milka and Gabriel (233). Her resolution to leave the city is an individualistic one, understandable because she is only an adolescent unable to change the existing customs in town. It shows, however, self-determination and sets up the contrast with her ancestors who were unable to break with the old establishment. She lives in a different world where that is more possible for a woman.

Bruna's leaving town proves irreversible and its irrevocable nature is conveyed again through magic, but this time, it is magic from the Catholic liturgy, from the Bible, a book of revelation which cannot be contested. Like most writers of *realismo maravilloso*, Yánez Cossío uses Biblical passages in ways which force a revision of their traditional interpretation. Bruna's experience reproduces and inverts the events narrated in the Bible. Tired of her running, Bruna turns her eyes to see the city and she does not find it, then she returns to the place she knew was the city but there is no trace of it. At this moment, the wind marvelously puts into her hands a verse from Genesis regarding the destruction of Sodom and Gomorrah:

> ...QUIERO IR Y VER SI SUS OBRAS IGUALAN AL RUMOR
> QUE HA LLEGADO A MIS OIDOS... (233)

In Genesis 19:24-25, Sodom and Gomorrah are destroyed when the Lord makes sulphur and fire rain upon the sinners' cities and in Genesis 19:26, Lot's wife is turned into a pillar of salt when she defies the Lord's order and turns to see the cities. Here, the city is destroyed but when Bruna turns around, the wind brings into her hands instead the explanation for that destruction. Contrary to the biblical scene where the woman is punished for trying to see what happens, defying the Lord's order, Bruna is given all the "knowledge" of the facts. Yánez Cossío is rewriting this Biblical passage, thus offering a "re-vision" of the canonical views of women which, "have constituted ideologies surrounding and defining women as evil, duplicitous, closer to nature, disallowed from speech, thought, or debate," to borrow the words of Rachel Blau DuPlessis (106-7). The "ciudad dormida" is ruled by cultural and religious myths. Bruna's attitude is an act of "resistance" to the impositions of her society.

Most of the action takes place in the house. When all women leave home to travel, they always return. The exception is Bruna. When she leaves town it is for good. After she leaves, the city is consumed by fire. There was no hope in her town, Bruna's individualistic solution was her only alternative to survive. By setting fire to the city until it disappears, Yánez Cossío sends an explicit message. The only way to build a society that gives men and women equal opportunities for their development is by destroying oppressive cultural myths.

Apart from the women in the family, there is Mama Chana, the old servant of the house. Mama Chana contributes to Bruna's knowledge and understanding of the past. In the house Bruna's favorite refuge are the back rooms where she finds objects that help her to reconstruct the story of her family. Bruna values the past and loves the old servant despite her faults (224).

The age of Mama Chana is never stated, but obviously she is more than a centenarian, for she has witnessed all the family events from the cruelty of María Illacatu's husband (28) to Bruna's days. Thanks to her marvelous longevity, Mama Chana knows all of the secrets of the family. Thus she decides to take advantage of the situation. When "tío Francisco" is dying, she makes him sign a document stating that all her illegitimate children were his own (125). Mama Chana's illegitimate children exemplify a well known situation in Latin America during colonial times when the "patrón" abused servants and never acknowledged his children.

With these nine female characters woman emerges as a "historical construct" of society. The diegetic rhetoric is constructed through the repetition of restrictive circumstances of women in every generation and of their confinement to the house, which is the "woman's place."

Yánez Cossío succeeds in presenting woman as a creation of a society where male dominance prevails but there is much more in the novel. Different cultural myths, such as religion, race, class, family system, pass through the sieve of her writing exposing social prejudices. She states that:

> El mito es la respuesta para hacerse dueño de las situaciones difíciles y de dominar las circunstancias. En nuestras sociedades, los mitos no son meros relatos, sino realidades vivientes. En *Bruna* trato de que los mitos sean tomados como tales y no como dogmas porque nadie puede vivir sin mitos, pero de todas formas ataco a los mitos religiosos, sociales, familiares.[12]

One important aspect to consider is how the father's name has been eliminated from the story. We only know him as "el marido" in María Illacatu's story; "el hijo mayor," as the father of Carmela and Teresa; Teresa's husband is never mentioned. Although we know the name of Bruna's grandfather we don't know what her father's name is. This absence of name serves a double purpose, on the one hand, it suggests the importance of men, their "social role" and predominance in society. It is the father who has the power and the authority. On the other hand, it is a textual strategy to undermine that same power and authority.

Obsession with religion is suggested all through the novel and is reinforced with one character, Salomón de Villacató, famous Bishop of the city, Bruna's grandfather. There is a strong criticism blended with fine irony

---

[12]From an interview with the author, in Quito, during the Summer, 1986.

in the bishop's marvelous story and blind religion becomes a myth. Salomón studies abroad and returns to the city as a bishop, hero of faith and religion (101). To save the city from Masonry, he decides to have an army formed by his own children. Hence he installs a nursery near the bishopric and personally takes care of the education of his two hundred and forty-five children whose mothers are the most highly considered ladies of society:

> Todo el saber del obispo se volcó en ellos... Formaban una orden militar y religiosa inspirada en la de los caballeros de las Cruzadas. Cuando recibieron las órdenes menores y el grado de tenientes, fueron designados con el nombre de "Batallón de la Fe". (104)

According to tradition of mores only men receive education, thus the Bishop keeps only the boys, the girls are given to their mothers. Women cooperate willingly in this noble cause of religion. Men do not agree at the beginning, but later, when the bishop convinces them of their wives' purity, they put forth no objections (105). Religion and the abuses often committed in its name are given a marvelous perspective. Real and marvelous isotopies are treated in identical form. Nobody questions the legitimacy of the "Batallón de la Fe;" what counts is the bishop's word. Irony is reinforced at the end of the story when the city is freed from the Bishop's tyranny one Resurrection Sunday. All men of the "Batallón" are killed and the Bishop, defeated, leaves town (108).

Social prejudices are treated within the family system, powerful in Latin America.[13] In this novel Bruna's family is the microcosm that reproduces society in general. Yánez Cossío's treatment of social taboos in the family is an effective way of attacking the social establishment. Problems of class and race are treated through changes in the last name of Bruna's family: the first children in Spain eliminate the name García and keep the maternal last name, Villacatu, which gives them prestige due to their mother's fortune. Back in America, to have an Indian ancestor is not regarded well. Thus Bruna's relatives gradually change their last name from Villacatu to Villa-Cató and finally to Catovil (25). Like Bruna's family, all families in the city arrange their genealogical trees at their convenience, always eliminating the Indians. This is a strong criticism against colonial stratification:

---

[13]Elizabeth Kuznesof and Robert Oppenheimer see the family in Latin America as the "central complex of relationships through which political, entrepreneurial, and agrarian history may be viewed to make societal sense out of seemingly impersonal phenomena" in "The Family and Society in Nineteenth-Century Latin America" (220).

Todos los habitantes de la ciudad tenían un árbol genealógico; podían, además darse el lujo de podarlo y de regarlo de tarde en tarde... Pero cuando aparecía un indio...podaban la rama del árbol y el indio caía a tierra y servía de abono. (23)

Another preoccupation is the cult of "honra." In this narrative the oldest son of María Illacatu loses his life defending his "honra." He does not want to give up his right to sit first, symbol of his social status, in the best seat of the bullfight: "el tatarabuelo de Bruna se fue al otro mundo con la celeridad de un relámpago...y el otro se quedó sin oreja y con su honra" (51). A third person narrator describes the situation and then criticizes the general ambience of the city where nobility is the excuse for many injustices:

La vanidad de las gentes de la ciudad y de los antecesores de Bruna seguirían por años y años encubando rencores, envidias, crímenes que se cometían y quedaban impunes... El culto a la llamada nobleza era una superstición que los mantenía ahogados. (51)

Colonial stratification is also reflected in work conditions. Labor is a discredit for the noble society therefore only the Indians work. None of María Illacatu's children work (86).

Men develop instead particular "hobbies." Marvelous and real elements are used to criticize social mores. The pastime of Alvarito de Villa-Cató, first grandson of María Illacatu, is to knit an extraordinary red rug for the Pope's visit to the city. He lacks exercise and becomes deformed. When he dies, twenty men, all from his family, carry the huge coffin and the rug unrolls itself to cover the way from his room to the church and then to his grave in the cemetery (92-93). People react naturally to this marvelous event and help to arrange the rug on the streets of the city:

Todos los habitantes de la ciudad ayudaron a los familiares a extender la alfombra sobre el empedrado de las calles, movidos por la curiosidad de ver hasta dónde llegaba. (93)

Five years later, the rug is destroyed by the weather and people develop chronic cold due to the fine dust coming from the rug. Women have to change their style and wear long skirts with huge pockets (bolsicones; they use sheets instead of handkerchiefs) where they can hide "hasta el fruto de amores clandestinos" (95). Here again, there is no conflict or transition between the real and marvelous isotopies. The insertion of the marvelous (Alvarito's weight, the rug's extension, the dust) in the real lexical paradigm is mixed with a series of trivial actions to rest importance to the supernatural. The logic of the discourse is maintained although there is no logic in the referential system.

There is no sign of perplexity among people for the extraordinary things, they simply adapt to the circumstances.

Jerónimo, Alvarito's youngest brother, devotes his time to frogs. After his death nobody takes care of them and the frogs invade the city. This invasion lasts several months (96-100). As usual, people react to the situation naturally, they feel uncomfortable and they simply comment that the frogs come from the Catovil's house. In Exodus 8:1-15 the Lord sends a plague of frogs to punish the Pharaoh's cruelty. In this text plagues come to the city due to blind beliefs and the inertness of people who accept everything without questioning.

Besides social criticism through individual characters like the above cases, there is also criticism denouncing the attitude of the community. This is done through "soroche," the metaphor used to depict all prejudices, injustices, and hypocrisies which predominate in the town. It is found everywhere; it is in the air of the city. "Soroche" plays a structural function and is represented in a visual way as fog, dust, or ashes. This atmosphere oppresses everybody, men, women and children. Thus there is no hope in "la ciudad dormida" and Bruna's decision is justified. Living far from her city she changes and enriches herself in contact with other people and other places. She continues, however, with her problem of noncommunication: "Pero vió que el mundo era un hervidero de pasiones y lo dejó todo" (236). Bruna's silence in this scene, when she is far from her home town and thus free from the "soroche," cannot be taken as a space of resistance before the power and the impositions of the other culture as was the case of her ancestor Maria Illacatu.

The last paragraph of the novel reads: "Los drogadictos, los sicodélicos, los rebeldes sin causa tardaron mucho tiempo en aparecer sobre la faz de la tierra..." (236).

This conclusion problematizes the diegesis and diminishes the force and potential of Bruna's escape, for instead of building something new she becomes a "desarraigada" (uprooted). Throughout the novel we have seen her as a determined and courageous girl who is able to break with old traditions and family impositions. She had enough reasons for her rebellion and we cannot take her as one of the "rebeldes sin causa" (236). She found her courage in the discovery of her Indian roots, "Soy yo, ahora..." (12), but this was not enough. Yet, although proud of her cultural heritage, Bruna, to the very end, seems to be condemned to lack of communication and thus to solitude.

In this text there is not a satisfactory resolution of *realismo maravilloso* as an homologous approach to the ideology of the "discurso americanista" such as we have seen in *Siete lunas y siete serpientes* where there is hope for *Santorontón* in "mestizaje." However, Yánez Cossío's novel provides space for a feminist discourse by reviewing woman's social status in a critical and dialectical manner. Her text makes the reader reflect that in order to have hope in cultural "mestizaje" male/female social inequities have to be resolved first.

The two novels analyzed in this chapter are an example of the uses of *realismo maravilloso* as a cultural referent in the Ecuadorian narrative of men and women in the 1970s. Aguilera Malta treats a universal problem, that of good and evil, questioning abuses of power. He uses *Santorontón* as a metaphor for Latin America. His oppositions of good/evil and "civilized" world/indigenous world render account of this problematic in the diegesis. Yánez Cossío uses Bruna's family as a metaphor for the society in the Andean Indian region, reviewing several of its cultural myths based on gender, class, and race. Her oppositions, man/woman, white/Indian, freedom/repression also serve her purposes in the diegesis.

In Aguilera Malta's work the marvelous is used in the sense of supernatural and the isotopies natural/supernatural appear systematically at all levels in any chapter and are maintained throughout the novel up to a satisfactory resolution at the end. In Yánez Cossío's work, the marvelous as supernatural appears particularly in María Illacatu's story. In the other parts of the novel the marvelous is treated mainly as the unusual in order to cast critical light on social mores. It has also a parodic intent which at times verges on the absurd.

Baroque descriptiveness is skillfully treated at all levels in Aguilera Malta's novel in enunciation, representation and language. Yánez Cossío's use of baroque is noted in the problematization of representation. Aguilera Malta recreates myths still believed by the indigenous population: faith in the afterworld, the brotherhood of man and nature, the pact with the devil and the belief in witches and evil spirits. Yánez Cossío denounces myths created by a classist and colonially restricted society and imposed by religion and family.

The ideologeme of "mestizaje" which is seen as the cultural symbiosis of Latin America in the "discurso americanista" triumphs in the work of Aguilera Malta, and the couple Candelario/Dominga seem to bring hope for peace and justice to the entire village. In Yánez Cossío's work, Bruna is not the solution for the city; her individualistic option does not change the mores of her town. As stated before, Bruna's attitude shows her nonconformity to the establishment that reduces the world of women to the domestic sphere of the house, always trying to conform to codes imposed by patriarchal power. The opposition is such that there is no hope for change.

These two solutions reflect differences faced by men and women under social pressures. Yánez Cossío's work addresses important social issues from a feminist perspective. Her critical and dialectical review of the status of women in society questions the female's role as portrayed in the other novels analyzed in this study. Yánez Cossío offers a rereading and reformulation of social problems in a society where patriarchal authority has always prevailed.

CONCLUSION

Alejo Carpentier, Gabriel García Márquez, José de la Cuadra, Demetrio Aguilera Malta, and Alicia Yánez Cossío use the discourse of *realismo maravilloso* in their works. Although narrative techniques have developed gradually from the 1930s on, nevertheless all of these writers have as a common preoccupation expressing in fiction the multifaceted and complex aspects of Latin American reality. Thus this mode has become a new way of writing which transcends the limits of the fantastic by entering the social realm. I have shown that José de la Cuadra's *Los Sangurimas* is a seminal work in this mode because of his innovative treatment of reality in a mythical world whose social, political, and economic development evolves around the dominance of a patriarch and his family over five generations. Many of the situations of this clan—the recurrence of incest, the madness of the patriarch, the revolutions led by his colonel—as well as social criticism are an anticipation of situations found in García Márquez's *Cien años de soledad*.

Writers in Latin America try to express the relationship between society and literature, but as Octavio Paz tells us in *One Earth, Four or Five Worlds*:

> The relationship between society and literature is not one of cause and effect. The link between the two is at once necessary, contradictory, and unpredictable. Literature expresses society; by expressing it, it changes, contradicts, or denies it. By portraying it, it invents it; by inventing it, it reveals it. (Paz 158)

By inventing such mythical places as *Macondo, La Hondura, Santorontón, La ciudad dormida*, the writers I have chosen for this study "reveal" "another reality." All portray social conflict and implicitly criticize injustice and oppression; each novel presents a closed world with its own laws, and each reflects the writer's own vision of a problematic reality and a deep preoccupation for his/her native culture and tradition.

There is intertextuality in these works, and general parallelism can be established. Besides the dominance of a family clan, the recurrence of incest, and the final madness of the patriarch, De la Cuadra and García Márquez present a complete cycle in the development of their closed worlds, from their creation to their end. But while in *La Hondura* destruction is suddenly foreseen after Nicasio's madness, in *Macondo* the reader witnesses each step of a gradual deterioration leading to its final destruction. In both cases, however, destruction comes when internal order is disrupted by exterior forces, the intervention of the Rural Police in *La Hondura* and the banana company in *Macondo*.

In Yánez Cossío's novel there is also a complete destruction of *La ciudad dormida*, similar to the destruction of Sodom and Gomorrah in *Genesis* 19:24, but there is a survivor, Bruna. There is devastation in Carpentier's *El reino de este mundo*, caused by a "great green wind," which is an antecedent to the apocalyptic hurricane that will destroy *Macondo* and the apocalyptic fire that will destroy *La ciudad dormida*. *Macondo*, *La Hondura*, *Santorontón*, and *La ciudad dormida* are mythical places that self-destruct and that make us think of the ancient myth of the destruction of a previous world followed by a new creation and the establishment of a Golden Age referred to by Mircea Eliade in *Aspects du mythe*. The message communicated to the reader is that it is necessary to eliminate social injustice for the creation of a better world.

Another common trait in the novels is the search for identity. In *La Hondura* Nicasio reconstructs his origins; in *El reino de este mundo* Ti Noel has a constant preoccupation with his African ancestors; in *Macondo* the search for identity is the preoccupation of the whole family, and this search for family identity is also a search for national and cultural identity (S. Jill Levine, *El espejo hablado* 29). In *Santorontón* the wizard Bulu-Bulu traces his origins to his African forebears, and in Yánez Cossío's novel Bruna is obsessed with her genealogy. Search for cultural identity has been a constant in the literature of Latin American writers since the beginning of the century.

Finally, as it was observed in each work, all present the juxtaposition of real and marvelous isotopies and the intersection of myth with sociohistorical conditions. These juxtapositions besides working into the poetic of marvelous realism also call for a reaction on the part of the reader, especially if we understand reading as a dialogue between the reader and the text. As Claudio Guillén rightly comments in *Entre lo uno y lo diverso*, referring to H.R. Jauss's Reception Theory: "la actividad del escritor hace posible un proceso de comunicación en que él mismo, como hombre de carne y hueso, ya no interviene; y cuyo desenlace está en manos de sus lectores... El acontecimiento resulta, en última y decisiva instancia, del encuentro de la obra con los códigos de los lectores" (Guillén 402-3). The writers of marvelous realism succeed not only in moving the reader to become interested in the different social problems they expose, but also in eliciting a social response.

The development of marvelous realism is shown both in narrative techniques and in social implications. While *Los Sangurimas* denounces the problem of latifundium, which predominated not only in Ecuador but in Latin American countries in general, and *El reino de este mundo* deals with social injustice in specific moments of Haitian history, *Cien años de soledad* multiplies its implications, and, as noted in our analysis, it is not possible to reduce the novel to one particular problem. When analyzing the banana company for example, the significance of the oppression is as true for Colombia as for any other Latin American country under neocolonialism. This aim to expand the scope of social connotations was also observed in *Siete lunas y siete serpientes* whose presentation of social problems as the eternal fight of the forces of good and evil has universal implications. Moreover, contrary to the devastation portrayed in *Macondo* and *La ciudad dormida*, there is a message of hope in Aguilera Malta's *Santorontón*. At the end of this novel, as noted above, the established order of despotism and corruption is foreseen, if not to be completely destroyed, at least to have a better balance in the future. Candelario Mariscal, the only one who can oppose the power of Chalena, will defend the cause of the poor, because among them is his fiancée, Dominga. Aguilera Malta's message of hope based on love is a distinctive factor that we do not find in the other novels studied. In *Siete lunas y siete serpientes*, love will finally bring hope for the community and will redeem the "races condemned to one hundred years of solitude," giving them a "second opportunity on earth." That opportunity is solidarity.

In *Bruna, soroche y los tíos* Yánez Cossío presents the social situation of women, and, although the novel refers to women of the Andean Indian region, it can also relate to the struggle of women in general. In all of these novels the message is "communicated" to the reader through the special use of language, which permits us to see the social underpinning of the magical surface. As was stated before, these works call for the participation of the reader to reflect on social issues and hopefully to act in search of a better world.

On a continent with such broad historical and social contrasts where the frontiers between the real and the imaginary are so close that it makes it difficult to distinguish one from the other, it seems natural that writers use this style as a means of expressing Latin American complexities as well as showing the need for questioning and affirming cultural identity.

Realismo maravilloso allows to be treated in literature, as extratextual referent, the numerous Latin American cultural elements referred to as "contexts" by Alejo Carpentier: racial, economic, chthonian, political, bourgeois, geographical, cultural, culinary, luminous, ideological. The five writers chosen for this study explore these contexts in an effective way and help the reader to better understand Latin American diversity and the essential need for change in the social structure.

SELECTIVE BIBLIOGRAPHY

Primary Sources

Aguilera Malta, Demetrio. *Don Goyo*. Madrid: Cenit, 1933.
---. *La isla virgen*. México, D.F.: Editorial Grijalbo, 1978.
---. *Siete lunas y siete serpientes*. México, D.F.: Fondo de Cultura Económica, 1970.
---. *Teatro completo*. México, D.F.: Finisterre, 1970.
Carpentier, Alejo. *Cuentos completos*. Barcelona: Bruguera, 1981.
---. *La novela latinoamericana en vísperas de un nuevo siglo*. México, D.F.: Siglo XXI Editores, 1981.
---. *Los pasos perdidos*. 5a ed. México, D.F.: Colección Ideas, 1968.
---. *Razón de ser*. La Habana: Editorial Letras Cubanas, 1980.
---. *El reino de este mundo*. 8a ed. Barcelona: Biblioteca Breve de Bolsillo, Seix Barral, 1980.
---. *Tientos y diferencias*. Montevideo: Edición Arca, 1967.
Cuadra, José de la. *Obras completas*. Intro. A. Pareja Diezcanseco. Ed. and notes J. Enrique Adoum. Quito: Casa de la Cultura Ecuatoriana, 1958.
García Márquez, Gabriel. *Cien años de soledad*. 35a ed. Buenos Aires: Editorial Sudamericana, 1973.
---. "Fantasía y creación artística en América Latina y el Caribe." *Texto crítico* 14 (1979): 3-8.
---. *Todos los cuentos*. Bogotá: Seix Barral, 1983.
Yánez Cossío, Alicia. *Bruna, soroche y los tíos*. 2a ed. Bogotá: Ediciones Paulinas, 1974.
---. *La casa del sano placer*. Quito: Editorial Planeta, 1989.
---. *La cofradía del mullo del vestido de La Virgen Pipona*. Quito: Editorial Planeta, 1985.
---. *Más allá de las islas*. Quito: Imprenta Don Bosco, 1980.
---. *Yo vendo unos ojos negros*. Quito: Casa de la Cultura Ecuatoriana, 1979.

Secondary Sources

Adoum, Jorge Enrique. *La gran literatura ecuatoriana del 30*. Quito: Editorial El Conejo, 1984.

---. "José de la Cuadra y el fetiche del realismo." *La bufanda del sol* 9-10 (febrero 1975): 27-34.

Aguilera Malta, Demetrio. "Diálogo con Fernando Alegría: novelas, novelistas y críticos." *Mundo nuevo* 56 (febrero 1971): 45-48.

---, Joaquin Gallegos Lara, and Enrique Gil Gilbert. *Los que se van. Cuentos del cholo y del montuvio*. Quito: Editorial El Conejo, 1985.

Ainsa Fernando. *Identidad cultural de Iberoamérica en su narrativa*. Madrid: Editorial Gredos, 1986.

Alazraki, Jaime. "Para una revalidación del concepto realismo mágico en la literatura hispanoamericana." 9-21. *Homenaje a Andrés Iduarte*. Clear Creek, Ind.: The American Hispanist, 1976.

Alegría Fernando. "Alejo Carpentier: realismo mágico." 92-125. *Literatura y revolución*. México, D.F.: Fondo de Cultura Económica, 1970.

---. *Nueva historia de la novela hispanoamericana*. Hanover, N.H.: Ediciones del Norte, 1986.

Altamirano, Carlos, and Beatriz Sarlo. *Literatura/sociedad*. Buenos Aires: Hachette, 1983.

Anderson Imbert, Enrique. "'Literatura fantástica', 'realismo mágico' y 'lo real maravilloso'." *Otros mundos otros fuegos* 39-44.

Arias Augusto. "Alicia Yánez y la novela." *El comercio* [Quito] (lunes 17 de abril de 1972): 4.

Astondoa, R. "Bruna, soroche y los tíos." *Letras del Ecuador* 153 (diciembre, 1972): 15.

Bakhtin, M.M. *The Dialogic Imagination*. Ed. Michael Holquist. Trans. Caryl Emerson and Michael Holquist. Austin: U Texas P, 1985.

Barrenechea, Ana María. "Ensayo de una tipología de la literatura fantástica." *Revista iberoamericana* 80 (julio-septiembre 1972): 391-403.

Barrett, Linton Tomás. "The Culture Scene in Ecuador: 1951." *Hispania* 35 (1952): 267-73.

Barriga López, Franklin. *Los mitos en la región andina*. Quito: Ediciones IADAP, 1984.

Barthes, Roland. "L'Effet de réel." *Communications* 11 (1968): 84-89.

---. *Mythologies*. Trans. Annette Lavers. New York: Hill and Wang, 1976.

Beauvoir, Simone de. *Le Deuxième Sexe*. Paris: Gallimard, 1949.

Bessière, Iréne. *Le Récit fantastique: la poétique de l'incertaine*. Paris: Larouse, 1974.

Borges, Jorge Luis. *El aleph*. 9a ed. Buenos Aires: Emecé, 1968.

---. "El arte narrativo y la magia." *Discusión*. 81-91. Buenos Aires: Emecé, 1961.

---. *Ficciones*. 26a ed. Buenos Aires: Emecé, 1978.

Braudel, Fernand. *On History*. Trans. Sarah Matthews. Chicago: U of Chicago P, 1980.

Cabrera, Vicente and Luis González-del Valle. *La nueva ficción hispanoamericana a través de M.A. Asturias y G. García Márquez*. New York: Eliseo Torres and Sons, 1972.

Campanella, Hortensia. "'No creo en la literatura de evasión'. Aguilera Malta, en España." *La gaceta*, suppl. of *El tiempo* [Quito] (domingo 15 de marzo de 1981): 2.

Campos, Haroldo de. "Superación de los lenguajes exclusivos." 279-300. *América Latina en su literatura*. Ed. César Fernández Moreno. México, D.F.: Siglo XXI, 1984.

Campos, Jorge. "Demetrio Aguilera-Malta y su saga mágica." *Insula* 302 (1972): 15.

Carrión, Benjamín. *El nuevo relato ecuatoriano*. Quito: Editorial Casa de la Cultura Ecuatoriana, 1958.

Carter, E. Dale. "Breve reseña del realismo mágico." xi-xv. *Ocho cuentos hispanoamericanos. Antología del realismo mágico*. New York: The Odyssey Press, 1970.

Cassirer, Ernst. *An Essay on Man*. New York: Bantam Books, 1970.

Castellanos, Rosario. *Balún Canán*. México, D.F.: Fondo de Cultura Económica, 1957.

---. *Mujer que sabe latín*. México, D.F.: Fondo de Cultura Económica, 1973.

---. *Oficio de tinieblas*. México, D.F.: Fondo de Cultura Económica, 1962.

Castex, Pierre-Georges. *Le Conte fantastique en France de Nodier à Maupassant*. Paris: Librairie José Corti, 1951.

Castro, Américo. *De la edad conflictiva. El drama de la honra en España y en su literatura*. Madrid: Taurus, 1961.

Chiampi, Irlemar. *O realismo maravilhoso: forma e ideologia no romance hispano-americano*. São Paulo: Editora Perspectiva, 1980.

Cixous, Hélène. "La Fiction et ses fantômes: une lecture de l'Unheimliche de Freud." *Poétique* 10 (1972): 199-216.

Communications 8 (1966).

Cornejo Polar, Antonio. *Sobre literatura y crítica latinoamericana*. Caracas: Ediciones de la Facultad de Humanidades y Educación, 1982.

Corrales, Manuel. "Las raíces del relato indigenista ecuatoriano." *Revista de crítica literaria latinoamericana* 4 (julio-agosto 1978): 39-52.

Costa, René de. "Reflexiones sobre el personaje de configuración mítica *vis a vis* la novela hispanoamericana dicha nueva." *Logos* 9 (junio de 1971): 48-53.

Courlander, Harold. *Haiti Singing*. New York: Cooper Square, 1973.

---. "Vodoun in Haitian Culture." 1-26. *Religion and Politics in Haiti*. Washington: Institute of Cross-Cultural Research, 1966.

Cueva, Agustín. "Ecuador: 1925-1975." 1.291-326. *América Latina: historia de medio siglo*. Ed. Pablo González Casanova. 6a ed. México, D.F.: Siglo XXI Editores, 1986.

---. "En pos de la historicidad perdida." *Revista de crítica literaria latinoamericana* 4 (julio-agosto 1978): 23-38.

---. *Lecturas y rupturas. Diez ensayos sociológicos sobre la literatura del Ecuador*. Quito: Editorial Planeta, 1986.

---. *La literatura ecuatoriana*. Buenos Aires: Centro Editor de América Latina, 1968.

---. "Literatura y sociedad en el Ecuador: 1920-1960." *Revista iberoamericana* 54 (julio-diciembre 1988): 629-647.

---. "Para una interpretación sociológica de *Cien años de soledad*." *Revista mexicana de sociología* 36.1 (1974): 59-76.

---. *El proceso de dominación política en el Ecuador*. México, D.F.: Ed. Diógenes, 1974.

Derrida, Jacques. *De la Grammatologie*. Paris: Minuit, 1967.

Díaz, Oswaldo. *El negro y el indio en la sociedad ecuatoriana*. Bogotá: Ediciones Tercer Mundo, 1978.

Diez, Luis A. "The Apocalyptic Tropics of Aguilera Malta." *Latin American Literary Review* 10 (Spring-Summer 1982): 31-40.

Donoso Pareja, Miguel. *Los grandes de la década del 30*. Quito: Editorial El Conejo, 1985.

Dorfman, Ariel. *Imaginación y violencia en América*. Santiago de Chile: Editorial Universitaria, 1970.

Dubois, J. et al. *Rhétorique génerale*. Paris: Larousse, 1970.

DuPlessis, Rachel Blau. *Writing Beyond the Ending*. Bloomington: Indiana U P, 1985.

Ecuador, pasado y presente. Ed. Instituto de Investigaciones Económicas. Quito: Crespo Encalada, 1982.

Eco, Umberto. *As formas do conteúdo*. Trans. P. de Carvalho. São Paulo: Perspectiva, 1974.

Eliade, Mircea. *Aspects du mythe*. Paris: Gallimard, 1963.

Engel, Paul. "Bruna, soroche y los tíos." *Letras del Ecuador* 155 (abril 1973): 23.

Fama, Antonio. "Entrevista con Demetrio Aguilera-Malta." *Chasqui* 7.3 (mayo 1978): 16-23.

---. *Realismo mágico en la narrativa de Aguilera Malta*. Madrid: Playor, 1977.

Febres Cordero, Francisco. "Con Aguilera Malta mientras sube la marea..." *La gaceta*, suppl. of *El tiempo* [Quito] (domingo 16 de agosto de 1981): 2.

Fernández Retamar, Roberto. *Para una teoría de la literatura hispanoamericana*. México, D.F.: Editorial Nuestro Tiempo, 1981.

Flores, Angel. "Magical Realism in Spanish American Fiction." *Hispania* 38.2 (mayo 1955): 187-92.

Foster, David William. *Alternate Voices in the Contemporary Latin American Narrative*. Columbia: U of Missouri P, 1985.

Fox, Arturo. "Realismo mágico: algunas consideraciones formales sobre su concepto." *Otros mundos otros fuegos* 53-56.

França Danese, Sérgio. Review of *O realismo maravilhoso. Forma e ideología no romance hispano-americano*, by Irlemar Chiampi. *Revista iberoamericana* 48 (enero-junio 1982): 442-47.

Friedmann de Goldberg, Florinda. Estudio preliminar a *El reino de este mundo*. Buenos Aires: Librería del Colegio, 1975.

Frye, Northrop. *Anatomy of Criticism*. Princeton: Princeton U P, 1973.

García Márquez, Gabriel, and Mario Vargas Llosa. *La novela en América Latina: diálogo*. Lima: Carlos Milla Batres, 1975.

Genette, Gérard. *Narrative Discourse. An Essay in Method*. Trans. Jane E. Lewin. Ithaca: Cornell U P, 1985.

Gilard, Jacques. "De *Los Sangurimas* a *Cien años de Soledad*." *Cambio* 8 (julio, agosto, septiembre 1977): 74-81.

González Echevarría, Roberto. *Alejo Carpentier: The Pilgrim at Home*. Austin: U of Texas P, 1990.

---. *The Voice of the Masters. Writing and Authority in Modern Latin American Literature*. Austin: U of Texas P, 1985.

González-Harvilan, Aída. "Comentarios sobre la novela *Bruna soroche y los tíos*, de Alicia Yánez Cossío." *El guacamayo y la serpiente* 19 (abril 1980): 51-71.

Granata, María. *Los viernes de la eternidad*. Buenos Aires: Emecé, 1971.

Greimas, A. J. "Élements pour une théorie de l'interpretation du récit mythique." *Communications* 8 (1966): 28-59.

Guevara, Darío. "Criollismo y folklore de *Bruna, soroche y los tíos.*" *Letras del Ecuador* 155 (abril 1973): 19.

Guillén, Claudio. *Entre lo uno y lo diverso. Introducción a la literatura comparada.* Barcelona: Editorial Crítica, 1985.

"Hacia una metodología de la apreciación literaria. Demetrio Aguilera en Quito." *Letras del Ecuador* 141 (enero de 1969): 23.

Halperín Donghi, Tulio. *Historia contemporánea de América Latina.* 10a ed. corr. y ampl. México, D.F.: Alianza Editorial Mexicana, 1983.

Heisse, Karl H. *El grupo de Guayaquil: arte y técnica de sus novelas sociales.* Madrid: Playor, 1975.

Hjelmslev, Louis. *Prolegomènes à une théorie du langage.* Trans. V. Canger. Paris: Minuit, 1971.

Icaza, Jorge. "Relato espíritu unificador en la generación del año 30." *Revista iberoamericana* 32 (julio-diciembre 1966): 211-16.

Jung, C.G. *Answer to Job.* Trans. R.F. Hull. Princeton: Princeton U P, 1973.

Koldwyn, Phillip. "Protesta guerrillera y mitológica: novela nueva de Aguilera-Malta." *Nueva narrativa hispanoamericana* 5 (1975): 199-205.

Kristeva, Julia. *Le Texte du roman.* Hague/Paris: Mouton, 1970.

Kuznesof, Elizabeth, and Robert Oppenheimer. "The Family and Society in Nineteenth-Century Latin America: An Historiographical Introduction." *Journal of Family History* (Fall 1985): 215-34.

Langer, Susanne K. *Philosophy in a New Key. A Study in the Symbolism of Reason, Rite, and Art.* New York: New York American Library, 1942.

Leal, Luis. "El realismo mágico en la literatura hispanoamericana." *Cuadernos americanos* 153 (julio-agosto 1967): 230-35.

Leante, César. "Confesiones sencillas de un escritor barroco." 11-31. *Homenaje a Alejo Carpentier: variaciones interpretativas en torno a su obra.* Ed. Helmy F. Giacoman. New York: Las Americas, 1970.

Levine, Suzanne Jill. *El espejo hablado. Un estudio de "Cien años de soledad."* Caracas: Monte Avila Editores, 1975.

---. "Lo real maravilloso": de Carpentier a García Márquez." *Revista de la cultura de occidente* 20 (1970): 563-76.

Lévi-Strauss, Claude. *Toteism.* Trans. Rodney Needham. Boston: Beacon Press, 1963.

---. *Anthropologie structurale.* 2 vol. Paris: Plon, 1958.

Leyburn, James G. *The Haitian People.* New Haven: Yale U P, 1966.

Lezama Lima, José. *La expresión Americana.* Madrid: Alianza Editorial, 1969.

Lotman, Jurij, et al. *Semiótica de la cultura*. Trans. Nieves Méndez. Ed. and notes Jorge Lozano. Madrid: Cátedra, 1979.

Ludmer, Josefina. *Cien años de soledad: una interpretación*. Santiago de Chile: Editorial Universitaria, 1972.

---. "Tretas del débil." In *La sartén por el mango*, 47-54.

Lugones, Leopoldo. *Antología de la prosa*. Buenos Aires: Ediciones Centurión, 1949.

Luzuriaga, Gerardo A. "Aguilera Malta se incorpora a la nueva narrativa." *Nueva narrativa hispanoamericana* 1.2 (1971): 219-24.

---. *Del realismo al expresionismo. El teatro de Aguilera-Malta*. Madrid: Plaza Mayor Ediciones, 1971.

Mabille, Pierre. *Le Miroir du merveilleux*. 2e. ed. Paris: Minuit, 1962.

Macdonell, Diane. *Theories of Discourse. An Introduction*. New York: Basil Blackwell, 1986.

Maldonado-Denis, Manuel. "Alejo Carpentier: literatura y sociedad caribeña." *Plural* 183 (diciembre 1983): 21-23.

Man, Paul de. *Blindness and Insight*. New York: Oxford U P, 1971.

Matté Blanco, Ignacio. *L'inconscio come insiemi infiniti*. Torino, Einaudi, 1981.

McBrien, Richard P. *Catholicism*. 2 vols. Minneapolis: Winston Press, 1980.

Mena, Lucila Inés. "Fantasía y realismo mágico." *Otros mundos otros fuegos* 63-68.

---. "Formulación teórica del realismo mágico." *Bulletin hispanique* 77 (1975): 395-407.

---. "La huelga de la compañía bananera como expresión de lo 'real maravilloso' americano en *Cien años de soledad*." *Bulletin hispanique* 74 (1972): 379-405.

Menton, Seymour. *Magic Realism Rediscovered, 1918-1981*. Philadelphia: Associated U P, 1983.

---. Review of "Siete lunas y siete serpientes." *Revista iberoamericana* 36 (octubre-diciembre 1970): 677-80.

Merrell, Floyd. "The Ideal World in Search of Its Reference: An Inquiry into the Underlying Nature of Magical Realism." *Chasqui* 4.2 (Feb. 1975): 5-17.

Métraux, Alfred. *Voodoo in Haiti*. Trans. Hugo Charteris. New York: Schocken Books, 1972.

Moreano, Alejandro. "Capitalismo y lucha de clases en la primera mitad del siglo XX." 137-224. *Ecuador: pasado y presente*. 2a. ed. Quito: Editorial Alberto Crespo Encalada, 1982.

Morello-Frosch, Marta. "El realismo integrador de *Siete lunas y siete serpientes*, de Demetrio Aguilera-Malta." *Otros mundos otros fuegos* 387-392.

Moreno, Hugo. *Introducción a la filosofía indígena*. Riobamba: Editorial Riobamba, 1983.

Naranjo, Carmen. *Mujer y cultura*. San José, C.R.: EDUCA, 1990.

O'Gorman, Edmundo. *La invención de América. El universalismo de la cultura de occidente*. México, D.F.: Fondo de Cultura Económica, 1958.

Ortiz, Gabriel. "El 'realismo mágico' de Demetrio Aguilera," *El universo* [Guayaquil] (domingo 16 de agosto de 1981): 18.

Ortiz, Fernando. *Hampa afro-cubana. Los negros brujos*. Madrid: Editorial América, 1917?

Otero, José. "Aguilera-Malta, Demetrio: *Siete lunas y siete serpientes*." *Hispania* 54 (1971): 404.

Otros mundos otros fuegos: fantasía y realismo mágico en Iberoamérica. Ed. Donald A. Yates. Memoria del XVI Congreso Internacional de Literatura Iberoamericana. East Lansing: Michigan State University: Latin American Studies Center, 1975.

Pareja Diezcanseco, Alfredo. *Ecuador, la república de 1830 a nuestros días*. Quito: Editorial Universitaria, 1979.

---. "Los narradores de la Generación del Treinta: El Grupo de Guayaquil." *Revista iberoamericana* 54 (julio-diciembre 1988): 691-707.

Parker, Alexander A. "Notes on the Religious Drama in Medieval Spain and the Origins of the "Auto Sacramental." *The Modern Language Review* 30 (April 1935): 170-82.

Paz, Octavio. *Corriente alterna*. México, D.F.: Siglo XXI, 1967.

---. *El laberinto la soledad*. 4a ed. México, D.F.: Fondo de Cultura Económica, 1964.

---. *One Earth, Four or Five Worlds*. Trans. Helen R. Lane. San Diego: Harcourt Brace Jovanovich, 1984.

---. *Tiempo nublado*. México, D.F.: Seix Barral, 1983.

Pontiero, Giovanni. "'The human comedy' in *El reino de este mundo*." *Journal of Inter-American Study and World Affairs* 12 (October 1970): 528-38.

Price-Mars, Jean. *La République d'Haïti et la République Dominicaine*. Tome I. Port-Au-Prince: L'Imprimerie Held, 1953.

Prince, Gerald. *A Dictionary of Narratology*. Lincoln: U of Nebraska P, 1987.

Quevedo, Francisco de. *El buscón I*. Ed. Américo Castro. Madrid: Espasa-Calpe, 1973.

118 Magic Realism: Social Context and Discourse

Rabassa, Clementine C. "El aire como materia literaria: la épica, la nueva narrativa, y Demetrio Aguilera-Malta." *Nueva narrativa hispanoamericana* 4 (1974): 261-68.

---. *Demetrio Aguilera-Malta and Social Justice.* Cranbury, N.J. Associated U P, 1980.

---. Review of *Siete lunas y siete serpientes*, by Demetrio Aguilera-Malta. *Books Abroad* 45 (1971): 285.

Rama, Angel. *Los dictadores latinoamericanos.* México, D.F.: Fondo de Cultura Económica, 1976.

---. *La novela en América Latina. Panorama 1920-1980.* Colombia: Colombiana, 1982.

---. *Transculturación narrativa en América Latina.* México, D.F.: Siglo XXI, 1982.

Ramón, Justo. *Historia de Colombia.* 10a ed. rev. Bogotá: Librería Stella, 1962.

Reyes, Oscar Efrén. *Breve historia general del Ecuador.* 5a ed. ampl. y corr. 2 tomos. Quito: Editorial "Fray Jodoco Ricke", 1957.

Ricci, Graciela N. *Realismo mágico y conciencia mítica en América Latina.* Buenos Aires: García Cambeiro, 1985.

Ricoeur, Paul. *La metáfora viva.* Milano: Jaca Book, 1981.

Riofrío, Miguel. *La emancipada.* Intro. Antonio Sacoto. Cuenca: Publicaciones del Departamento de Difusión Cultural, 1983.

Roa, Miguel F. "Alejo Carpentier tras diez años de silencio." *ABC* [Madrid] (2 de febrero de 1975): 28-31.

Robles, Humberto E. "Génesis y vigencia de Los Sangurimas." *Revista iberoamericana* 106-107 (enero-junio 1979): 85-91.

---. "La noción de vanguardia en el Ecuador." *Revista iberoamericana* 54 (julio-diciembre 1988): 649-74.

---. *Testimonio y tendencia mítica en la obra de José de la Cuadra.* Quito: Editorial Casa de la Cultura, 1976.

Rodó, José Enrique. *Obras completas.* 2a ed. Madrid: Aguilar, 1967.

Rodríguez Castelo, Hernán. "Demetrio Aguilera M., por él mismo." *El tiempo* [Quito] (domingo 23 de agosto de 1970): 26, 29.

Rodríguez Castelo, Hernán et al. *La literatura ecuatoriana en los últimos 30 años.* Quito: Editorial El Conejo, 1983.

Rodríguez Monegal, Emir. "Lo real y lo maravilloso en *El reino de este mundo.*" 102-32. *Asedios a Carpentier.* Ed. Klaus Müller-Bergh. Santiago de Chile: Editorial Universitaria, 1972.

---. "*One Hundred Years of Solitude*: The Last Three Pages." *Books Abroad* 47 (1973): 485-89.

---. "Realismo mágico versus literatura fantástica: un diálogo de sordos." *Otros mundos otros fuegos* 25-37.

Roh, Franz. "Realismo mágico." *Revista de occidente* 48 (1927): 274-301.

Rojas, F. Angel. *La novela ecuatoriana*. Guayaquil-Quito: Clásicos Ariel/Biblioteca de Autores Ecuatorianos, 1978.

Rosaldo, Michelle Zimbalist, and L. Lamphere. *Women, Culture and Society*. Stanford: Stanford U P, 1974.

Sacoto, Antonio. "La novela ecuatoriana del '70." *Cuadernos americanos* 230 (mayo-junio 1980): 200-209.

---. *La nueva novela ecuatoriana*. Cuenca: Departamento de Difusión Cultural, 1981.

Sainz de Medrano, Luis. *Historia de la literatura hispanoamericana: desde el modernismo*. Madrid: Taurus, 1989.

La sartén por el mango. Eds. Patricia Elena González, and Iliana Ortega. Río Piedras, P.R.: Huracán, 1985.

Schneider, David M. *American Kinship: A Cultural Account*. Englewood Cliffs, N.J.: Prentice Hall, 1968.

"6 nuevos libros ecuatorianos." *Letras del Ecuador* 154 (febrero, 1973): 3.

Simons, Marlise. "Love and Age: A Talk with García Márquez." *The New York Times Book Review*, 7 April 1985.

Speratti-Piñero, Emma Susana. *Pasos hallados en* El reino de este mundo. México, D.F.: El Colegio de México, 1981.

Theory and Practice of Feminist Literary Criticism. Eds. Gabriela Mora, and Karen S. Van Hooft. Ypsilanti, Mich.: Bilingual P, 1982.

Tobar García, Francisco. "Bruna no era centenaria." *El comercio* [Quito]. (miércoles 21 de marzo de 1973): 4.

Todorov, Tzvetan. *The Fantastic. A Structural Approach to a Literary Genre*. Cornell: Cornell U P, 1975.

---. "Macondo en París." *Texto crítico* 2 (1978): 44.

Uslar-Pietri, Arturo. *Letras y hombres de Venezuela*. Caracas: Ediciones Edime, 1958.

Valbuena Briones, Angel. "Una cala en el realismo mágico." *Cuadernos americanos* 166 (septiembre-octubre 1969): 233-41.

Valverde, María E. *La narrativa de Aguilera Malta: un aporte a lo real-maravilloso*. Guayaquil: Casa de la Cultura Ecuatoriana, 1979.

Vargas Llosa, Mario. *García Márquez: historia de un deicidio*. Barcelona: Seix Barral Editores, 1971.

---. "The Latin American Novel Today." *Books Abroad* 44:1 (Winter 1970): 7-16.

Vasconcelos, José. *La raza cósmica. Misión de la raza iberoamericana*. Madrid: Aguilar, 1966.

Vax, Louis. *L'Art et la literature fantastique*. Paris: P.U.F., 1970.

Villaveces, Jorge, ed. *Los mejores discursos de Jorge Eliécer Gaitán 1919-1948*. 2a. ed. Bogotá: Editorial Jorvi, 1968.

Volek, Emil. "Análisis evaluativo e interpretación de *El reino de este mundo*, de Alejo Carpentier." 145-78. *Homenaje a Alejo Carpentier*. Ed. Helmy F. Giacoman. New York: Las Americas, 1970.

White, Hayden. *Tropics of Discourse. Essays in Cultural Criticism*. Baltimore: Johns Hopkins U P, 1986.

Wolffsohn, Elisabeth. "Algunos aspectos del relato de Alicia Yánez Cossío." 333-80. *Situación del relato ecuatoriano. Nueve estudios*. Ed. Manuel Corrales Pascual. Quito: Centro de Publicaciones PUCE, 1977.

Xirau, Ramón. "Crisis del realismo." 202-203. *América Latina en su literatura*. Ed. César Fernández Moreno. México, D.F.: Siglo XXI, 1979.

INDEX OF AUTHORS CITED

Mallea, Eduardo 5
Man, Paul de xi
Mariátegui, José Carlos 11, 15
Martí, José 19
Martínez, Luis A. 48, 52, 65
Mata, G. h. 53n.7
Matté Blanco, Ignacio 15-17
McBrien, Richard P. 39n.9
Medvedev, N.P. 9n.2
Mena, Lucila Inés 6-7, 42n.10, 43
Menton, Seymour 3n.1
Mera Eduardo 48
Mera, Juan Leon 52n3
Merrell, Floyd 7
Métraux, Alfred 21n.3, 25, 26
Moran, Charles 29
Moreano, Alejandro 48n.1
Moreno, Hugo 96

Naranjo, Carmen 97n.11
Neuman, Erich 14

Onetti, Juan Carlos 20, 34
Oppenheimer, Robert 102n.13
Ortiz, Adalberto 51, 54n.8
Ortiz, Fernando 19, 59n.16
Ortner, Sherry B. 96n.10

Palacio, Pablo 51, 53n.7
Pareja Diezcanseco, Alfredo 50,
    51, 53, 53n.7, 54, 75
Parker, Alexander 82n.3
Paz, Octavio 11, 17, 20, 71, 106
Picón Salas, Mariano 19
Placide-Justin 27
Pontiero, Giovanni 25
Price-Mars, Jean 24
Prince, Gerald 18
Proust, Marcel 5

Puig, Manuel 34

Quevedo, Francisco de 59n.16

Rabassa, Clementine C. 81, 85n.5
Rabassa, Gregory 76n1
Ramón, Hno. Justo, S.C. 44
Reyes, Alfonso 19
Reyes, Oscar Efrén 50
Ricci, Graciela N. xii, 8, 13, 14,
    15, 16, 17, 18, 19n1
Ricoeur, Paul 13
Riofrío, Miguel 52
Rivadeneira, Jorge 75
Rivera, José Eustasio 31, 59n.16
Roa, Miguel F. 32
Roa Bastos, Augusto 34, 50
Robles, Humberto E. 57n.12,
    58n.15, 59n.16, 65, 70
Rodó, José Enrique 11, 15, 19
Rodríguez Castelo, Hernán 88
Rodríguez Monegal, Emir 5, 17,
    34
Roh, Franz 3, 5-6
Rojas, F. Angel 11, 49, 50, 53n.6,
    53n.7, 54n.8
Rosaldo, Michelle Zimbalist
    96n.10
Rulfo, Juan 20

Sábato, Ernesto 34
Sacoto, Antonio 52n3, 58n.15, 75
Saint Méry, Moreau 21n.3
Salvador, Humberto 53n.7
Sánchez, Luis Alberto 17, 49
Sainz de Medrano, Luis 50n.2
Sarduy, Severo 34
Sarmiento, Domingo F. 11, 15
Schatz, Barry 27